SOME POEMS/POETS

Also by Samuel Charters

Poetry

Plays

Music

Some Poems /Poets

by Samuel *Barclay* Charters

with photographs by Ann Charters

Studies in	Oyez
American	•
Underground	Berkeley
Poetry	•
Since 1945	1971

Copyright © 1971 by Samuel Charters

Book design by Cranium Press

First Edition

for Charles Olson

> The distances of those eyes,
> out of the face on the stale pillow,
> the distances of the fingers   opening
>   to reach out the hand to mine.
>
> " . . . I wanted to tell you I
> finished the Maximus.   I dunnow.   Maybe
> I blew it finishing it . . ."
>
> What began out of those eyes, Charles?
> How do we begin again
>   without those eyes?

Contents

An Introduction

I don't want anyone who's interested in contemporary poetry to be put off by any sense of formality in these studies of a group of poems and poets out of the last twenty years of the American poetic experience. Even "study" is too serious a term for what are simply loose responses to some of the implications of the poetry. I'm not trying to explain anything - not American poetry, and not these poems or poets. I think that explaining a creative act leads away from the moment of the act - that the explanation begins to take on its own kind of importance - and what I want to do is lead to the poem, to the poet - to the experience of the poem itself. The problem with American poetry today isn't that it's difficult or abstract or removed from reality - the only problem is that it isn't read enough. What I've tried to do in these studies is to get down some of my own responses to writing that seems to have an importance in the growth of the new American poetry - with the intention that this kind of opening to an experience of the poem might lead someone to the poem itself.

I use the word important - but only because I think that either the poet has written a body of work that has had a strong influence on other poets, or that the poem itself is a strong expression of an attitude shared by a number of other writers. Charles Olson, or Robert Creeley, certainly have had such a strong influence on a number of younger poets that they would have to be included in any kind of response to contemporary poetry. Poets like Lew Welch or Jack Spicer aren't as widely read, but often their work centers on an attitude or an involvement toward poetry or the society that seems to represent the thinking of a number of other poets. I don't think of any of the writing as "good" or "bad" in the usual critical sense. Certainly there has to be a positive response to the poem, but I don't think that the usual necessity for a "critical judgement" is important to this kind of loose response. Statements like "the most important writer in English today," or "the dominant influence on a generation of American poets," I think mean that the person writing them isn't really interested in poetry - just in literary history, which is something different. These poets are writing poetry now, I am reading them now, and each of them expresses some aspect of the now that involves us all. I think that is what poetry should do - that it's what these poets are doing.

It's misleading, in some ways, to think of these poets as part of an "underground" poetical movement; since that implies a similarity of attitudes that for most of them isn't there. But in one way they have to be thought of as underground in contrast to the "visible" poetry of the academic writers. The poets who more or less derive from the Anglo-American literary background - usually most evident in a strong affinity for Yeats - dominate the world of the literary journal and the university lecture, and since there isn't much other serious interest in poetry anywhere else in the academic community their dominance in these areas gives them a large prominence. The underground poets have had to scramble for publication in small, often fugitive magazines or anthologies, they've had to print each other's poems - Ferlinghetti's City Lights Press or Creeley's Divers Press - and, so far, they've had to rely on each other for any serious discussion and criticism. Despite all of this, they've still managed to reach a genuine audience for their work -

an audience of readers who believe in the poem as a living, vital expression, rather than as an object in the stream of literary history. Ferlinghetti is one of the best selling poets in the United States today, and Allen Ginsberg's *Howl* was, by any commercial standards, a best selling book. There has been almost no critical attention paid to the work of Olson or Robert Duncan - the study *Olson/Melville, A Study in Affinity*, in 1968, was the first extended examination of the work of either of them - but their books are published and their work is being read. Collections of their work have been in print continuously for nearly twenty years and there is a steadily widening response to their poetry.

In one sense the term "underground" does suit most of them, with its sense of political alienation. They are, often, angrily idealistic, and their questioning of the American social ethos has been an embarrassment to certain levels of the American establishment. The traditionally oriented poets, even though they often agree with the political attitudes of the underground, lack the real anger of disappointment. They have learned, from Yeats and Eliot, to be disaffected. Disaffection is not to be expected from Allen Ginsberg or Ferlinghetti. They have chosen to step outside the values and attitudes of society, and their act, in itself, has committed them to an involvement in social ideals. In part, their audience is drawn to them for this idealistic withdrawal, and this is the only true audience a poet can have, people reading his work because of its reflection of their own emotional reality. There is a conscious, articulate underground in contemporary American society, and it is these poets who write their poetry.

I don't think literary history is important in the relationship between these poems and somebody wanting to read them, but here, in an introduction, some of the background might be useful. A history of the poetic output isn't too meaningful; since all of them have been writing at the same time (with the exception of Jack Spicer, who died in 1965), most of them are about the same age, and they have a strong personal influence on each other. But it is useful to realize that their affinities to the immediately older generation of poets have been generally built on political bases, rather than aesthetic - usually those poets who were also American idealists, angry and disappointed at the failure of the American social dream. Of the most obvious of the poets of the 1920's and 1930's many were politically uncongenial. Cummings was a snob, Eliot an elitist and troubled Christian convert, Frost - as well as Sandburg and MacLeish - became an American apologist, and Jeffers' "blood myth" was considered fascistic. But Pound and William Carlos Williams both had a strong political motivation and a definite artistic attitude, and each has been important in the background of the new American poetry. Pound's disappointment in western society finally led him to a confused acceptance of the government of Italy's Mussolini, which was certainly fascist, but - among poets - there has been little criticism. In a way his motivation was acceptable - stemming from a genuine idealism - and Italian fascism, unlike German, was so inept there is - in retrospect - almost a grim humor about it. Certainly the early Pound - of "Hugh Selwyn Mauberly" - is still one of the strongest expressions of the contemporary disillusion.

From Pound has come the sense of larger structure and the ability to organize larger clusters of material, as well as an involvement in the romantic grandeur of medieval and early Renaissance poetry. Pound's forms - attitudes -

> Who even dead, yet hath his mind entire!
> This sound came in the dark
> First must thou go the road
> > to hell
> And to the bower of Ceres' daughter Proserpine,

Through overhanging dark, to see Tiresias,
Eyeless that was, a shade, that is in hell
So full of knowing that the beefy men know less than he,
Ere thou come to the road's end . . .
                              The small lamps drift in the bay
And the sea's claws gathers them.
Neptunus drinks after neap-tide.
Tamuz!   Tamuz!
The red flame going seaward. . . .   (*Canto XLVII*)

are used as structural elements again and again. In Olson,

They buried their dead in a sitting posture
Serpent   cane   razor   ray of the sun

And she sprinkled water on the head of the child, crying
"Cioa-coatl!   Cioa-coatl!"
with her face to the west

Where the bones are found, in each personal heap
with what each enjoyed, there is always
the Mongolian louse

The light is in the east. Yes. And we must rise, act. Yet
in the west, despite all the apparent darkness (the whiteness
which covers all), if you look, if you can bear, if you can, long
                              enough   (*The Kingfisher*)

in Duncan,

        Psyche's tasks - the sorting of seeds
    wheat   barley   oats   poppy   coriander
    anise   beans   lentils   peas   - every grain
            in its right place
                              before nightfall;
    gathering gold wool from the cannibal sheep
    (for the soul must weep
        and come near upon death);
    harrowing Hell for a casket Prosperina keeps
                              that must not
        be opened, containing beauty?
    no!   melancholy coild like a serpent

                    that is deadly asleep
        we are not permitted
                to succumb . . . (*A Poem Beginning With A Line*
                            By Pindar)

and in the younger poets who have taken their Pound
through the work of older men like Olson and Duncan.

William Carlos Williams' influence has been in the
short, almost laconic poem phrase, and in a kind of short
poem in which he isolated a moment of experience. In
Williams the poem could be only a glimpse,

    Monday
            the canna flaunts
    its crimson head

    crimson lying folded
    crisply down upon

                the invisible

    darkly crimson heart
    of this poor yard . . .

                            (*The Descent of Winter*)

the mood has been picked up by other poets, among them
Creeley,

    Some echoes,
    little pieces,
    falling, a dust,

    sunlight, by
    the window, in
    the eyes. Your

    hair as
    you brush
    it, the light

    behind
    the eyes,
    what is left of it.   (*Some Echoes*)

Denise Levertov,

> The washing hanging from the lemon tree
> in the rain
> and the grass long and coarse
>
> Sequence broken, tension
> of bitter orange sunlight
> frayed off.
>   So light a rain
> pending above the rigid leaves . . . (*The five-Day Rain*)

And in many of the poets there is also some of Hart Crane's verbal density, an occasional unconscious reflection of Marianne Moore's affection for exotic language, a response to Wallace Stevens' hard brilliance.

In all of these poets there is a complete acceptance - almost without questioning - of the necessity of a poetry that uses the rhythms and the idioms of the spoken language, and of the reality of Emerson's statement "For it is not metres, but metre-making argument, that makes a poem, a thought so passionate and alive, that, like the spirit of a plant or an animal, it has an architecture of its own . . ." Olson, in his essay "Projective Verse"- which Williams considered important enough to include almost in its entirety in his autobiography - makes an attempt to schematize the new poetic idiom but Olson's "principle," despite his crediting it to Creeley, has a more clearly identifiable source.

> (2) is the *principle*, the law which presides conspicuously over such composition, and, when obeyed is the reason why a projective poem can come into being. It is this: FORM IS NEVER MORE THAN AN EXTENSION OF CONTENT. (Or so it got phrased by one, R. Creeley, and it makes absolute sense to me, with this possible corollary, that right form, in any given poem, is the only and exclusively possible extension of content under hand.) There it is, brothers, sitting there for use.

It is, of course, simply a re-phrasing of Emerson's comment on "metre-making argument." Earlier in the essay Olson makes a more general statement that is perhaps a clearer indication of what he is describing.

> Verse now, 1950, if it is to go ahead, if it is to be of *essential* use, must, I take it, catch up and put into itself certain laws and possibilities of the breath, of the breathing of the man who writes as well as of his listenings.

Most of the poets accept this without thinking, and perhaps because of this, despite their influence on each other, they don't write alike. They believe that the poem is an expression of their own breath and speech and thought, and their poetry is as different as the poets are different from each other as people. And there is, as well, the strong identification with the emotional liberalism that has its roots in the American transcendental idealism of the 19th Century. In some ways perhaps the most compelling "poem" of the 1950's - expressing the deep validity of this idealism, as well as what has been, in the United States today, its disappointment - is Jack Kerouac's novel *On The Road*. The book's last glimpse of its romantic idealist, Dean Moriarty, standing broke, cold, and sick on a winter New York street, could symbolize the position of this group of American poets, who feel an angry alienation from the society that involves them so passionately.

It could be argued that since most of this poetry still has only a kind of underground existence that it has no importance in the aesthetic culture of American society. This could even be true. At no place in the society is there a deep emotional involvement with poetry that could match the excitement over movies or rock and roll - even if it's a poet like Ferlinghetti or Ginsberg, whose books have strong sales. But the poetry of any society is finally one of the few things that continue to have a creative impetus, that become

the shaping force of a new emerging society. In a true sense
poetry, in itself, is important. As Williams wrote in "Asphodel, That Greeny Flower,"

> It is difficult
> to get news from poems
>   yet men die miserably every day
>   for lack
> of what is found there.

Charles Olson

The Maximus Poems - "letter 7"

> I am caught
>
> in Gloucester. (What's buried
> behind Lufkin's
> Diner? Who is
>
> Frank Moore?
>
> *(The Librarian)*
>
> And I am asked - ask myself (I, too covered
> with the gurry of it) where
> shall we go from here, what can we do
> when even the public conveyances
> sing?
>
> *(The Songs of Maximus)*
>
> The trouble is, it is very difficult, to be both a poet
> and, an historian -
>
> *(The Mayan Letters)*

It is difficult - awkward - to make this kind of evaluation, but Charles Olson, I think, has to be considered one of the strongest influences, one of the most decisive forces, on an entire area of modern American poetry. No one seems to quite measure up his size, despite the brilliance and the uniqueness of much of the writing around him. It's a sense of size and in some ways even more important a sense of place, a sense of being placed. American poetry comes out of a society that is uncertain and uneasy and the poetry has always had some of this uneasiness - not even developing traditions or any strong sense of direction. It always seems to be beginning, and every poet seems to be the beginning of a new American poetry. Olson, with his sense of having found a place, has the range and the strength to be a force - in his own way to be this kind of beginning, this kind of new American poet.

I think the feeling of place has to go beyond a personal focus. The first place a poet has to find is the ground he stands on - then he has to go out and find the distances to the places where other poets have decided to stand - to the place where they stand in the culture, and the place they stand in the society. Many contemporary poets have gotten to the first step. It's the larger vision of a place in the culture and the society that's beyond them. Olson got this far very early - partly by borrowing much of his early poetic stance and technique from Ezra Pound. There are early poems, important early writing, that could almost be unnumbered Cantos - "The Kingfishers" or "The Praises." Robert Duncan, whose work has sometimes been associated with Olson's, like him also has this strong affinity for Pound and some of his work - "A Poem Beginning With a Line By Pindar," sections from "Passages" - could also have been added to the Cantos. Olson found in Pound a feeling for the sweep of a culture and an angry alienation from some of the worst aspects of the American experience, and for him it was a beginning. Olson began writing late - in his middle thirties - so Pound was of considerable use to him. There is still, in almost all of Olson's poetry, a suggestion of Pound's technical devices and his artistic concerns. Pound opened him out and set him going and the feeling for Pound and his grasp of the poem will always be with Olson.

But with this strong connection there are still strong feelings of difference between the two men, especially as Olson's work has matured. There is no strong sense of place in Pound's work, despite his sentimental attachments to

Italy and the troubadour poetry of Provence. His concern is with culture, with society as culture, and in the Cantos he has gone through everything he could reach to use as material. This has given him enormous range, but in trying to reach so much I feel that often he spreads himself too thin. He has an intellectual sense of identity with his materials, but there is often no sense of a significant emotional involvement. With Olson his identity with the place, with Gloucester, gives his major work, *The Maximus Letters*, a deep emotional center. The only other American writer who gives me the same sense of responding to a place, in both an historical and philosophic sense, is Thoreau in his first book, *A Week On The Concord And Merrimack Rivers*. He used the scene of the rivers and the fields and the mountains as a backdrop to his larger concern with the materials of colonial history and his own moral essays. Olson, in one of the Letters' most persistent themes, uses Gloucester as a poetic expression of the realities of history. Sometimes he has used materials similar to Thoreau's, and drawn some of the same inferences from similar documents, but in Thoreau there was always a sharp moral concern with the implications of his materials and he used them in the book to give an immediate clarity to his ideas. Olson, working in a larger concept that includes a whole new structure of the poem and of literature, is more ambiguous, but in some of the suggestions of his materials still as powerful.By not clearly forcing them into a place in the poem he has left them with their own interior force as document and history, instead of with the smaller place as example or illustration of some point. The structure and even some of the language of *The Maximus Letters* has been strongly influenced by William Carlos Williams' *Paterson*, but Williams' poem is an extended allegory involving the man and the city. In some of the early letters there is an extending of the figure of Maximus into an allegorical framework, but it's left as an ambiguous suggestion, and in the rest of the poem Maximus - Olson - stays at a distance from this kind of self-identification with Gloucester.

The sense of place in the Letters is - in a final sense - so compelling because what Olson is trying to hold on to is the sense of place in time, as well as the sense of the immediate place of Gloucester. In geometric terms he is developing place in vertical as well as horizontal planes. This gives the Letters a complex pattern of movement, as well as giving them some of their importance to contemporary poetry. It also gives them some of their difficulty. Sometimes the poetry has the clarity and the vividness - the loose, unconcerned line of the kind of American discourse that he so strongly defends and insists on.

> This morning of the small snow
> I count the blessings, the leak in the faucet
> which makes of the sink time, the drop
> of water on water as sweet
> as the Seth Thomas
> in the old kitchen
> my father stood in his drawers to wind

There are many passages in the Letters with this directness. It is, after all, Olson who wrote the essay "Projective Verse," with its insistence on the value of the poet's immediate expression. But more characteristic of the Letters is a complex style that involves his conception of history with his creative responses as a poet. Sometimes the association is close, directly from a moment of the poem.

> I sit here on a Sunday
> with grey water, the winter
> staring me in the face
>
> "the Snow lyes indeed
> about a foot thicke
> for ten weeks" John White
> warns any prospective
> planter

But in most of the Letters the history is the poem.
"So Sassafras" begins

> Europe just then was being drained swept by the pox so
> sassafras
> was what Ralegh Gosnold Pring only they found fish not cure

"Some Good News"

> how small the news was
> a permanent change had come
> by 14 men setting
> on Cape Ann, on the westerly side
> of the harbor

"On First Looking out through Juan de la Cosas's Eyes"

> Behaim - and nothing
> insula Azores to
> Cipangu (Candyn
> somewhere also there where spices

The Letters become less of the poet's expression and more the historian's as they go on, even though the history is handled as poetic material. In any of the single Letters the history is almost without meaning - odd facts, lists of provisions, inserted paragraphs on the fishing industry - but with the growth of the poem as a whole it is clear that something else is involved. The same facts return again and again. He goes back again and again to look at Gloucester from every view point that the town's history gives him. The impetus - he would call it "thrust"- is moral - a New England transcendental morality concerned with the destruction of the early American ideal by commercial growth.
From Letter 10

> (as I have been witness,
> in my time,
> to all slide
> national, international,
> even learning slide

Charles Olson 25

Letter 3

> The word does intimidate. The pay-check does.
> But to use either, as cheap men
>
> O tansy city, root city
> let them not make you
> as the nation is

It is a use of history beyond a recitation of names and dates, it is history as his - Charles Olson's - own experience.

Sometimes I find myself thinking of Olson as an artisan, a worker with his hands, a carpenter, a New England journeyman. The woodworkers who did the carvings, flutings, ceilings; ship carpenters who did the bowsprit figures, as well as the trim, railings, hatch covers, and hand gear. The sense of the work being finished, of being placed. It is difficult to be both a historian and a poet, but by using some of his materials as an artisan would he is usually able to keep the two together within the poem. His history, like the carpenter's plank, still has its own grain and smell when he gets through with it. And he uses more than history. There is a strong set of personal responses that also have become part of the Letters. In the earlier Letters there is a more open, more direct feel of language and image - even the simple, beautiful set of "The Songs Of Maximus." In the earlier sections it is much more Olson as artist that I feel - more poet than historian - the matter of the poetry coming out of someplace inside his own Gloucester experience. And the whole of the poem does seem to open out from the centering of himself in Gloucester, and from the feeling of himself within this place. In the earlier poems most of the themes that dominate the later have already been outlined, even if they have only been loosely threaded on the line of his own memories of the town's fishing fleet and the men of the boats.

Of the early Letters I think that Letter 7 opens up the longer themes in a full sense, while still keeping its own coherence as a separate poem. Olson as "I, Maximus" dominates the poem, as he does all of the early poems, but it is an open, expansive Olson. Already - and this is only the seventh Letter - there is so much cross reference that in many places it's necessary to go back to the earlier poems, but it's less difficult to approach than many of the other poems, since in a loose, casual way it's about something.

> (Marsden Hartley's
> eyes - as Stein's
> eyes

The fullest aspect of the poem is still its involvement with Gloucester, but it is also about the painter Marsden Hartley - the period of his work in Gloucester, the powerful, mythic, almost folk paintings of the 1930's. The emphasis of the Letter is still circular - within, from, and to Gloucester - but Olson has separated out a part of this experience, and given it a distinct, separate identity outside of the main currents of the rest of the Letters.

I've never decided whether or not Olson considers his poems difficult to follow - or if he cares, but he is difficult, one of the most difficult of the modern poets to follow. Sometimes, as in the inner references of Letter 7, it's because he doesn't give enough away - at other times, as in the overall structure of the Letters, because he includes a maze of only distantly related material. Probably, since he knows the inference of everything he's saying he doesn't see the difficulty at all. And even if he does see it the work is interrelated, and he could have decided that if he's opaque at one point the same reference will come up again at a point where the light hits it a little more strongly. But I want to try to follow some of the outlines of this Letter; since even the method of construction is an aspect of Olson as artisan/craftsman.

Charles Olson 27

Hartley's eyes were deeply drawn, haunting eyes - to begin with Hartley his eyes would be a good beginning - and since he was a painter his eyes are a tool - something of his craftsmanship. Stein? Helen Stein, a Gloucester painter who was a close friend of both Olson and Hartley. She has already been mentioned in the Letters - in Letter 5 - and it was her eyes, then, that Olson mentioned,

> Helen Stein's eyes, and those others, Gloucester, who look,
> who still can look

and the directness, the sureness of the glance that he felt in Hartley as well. Only the mention; then he's returned to his Gloucester fishermen - who are part of what he's trying to say about Hartley.

> Or that carpenter's,

(the carpenter's eyes)

> who left Plymouth Plantation,
> and came to Gloucester,
> to build boats

> and who owned the land of "the Cut",
> until Gloucester, too, got too proper
> and he left . . .

for twenty-three lines he goes back over the same historical ground that dominates much of the Letters, the first years of the Gloucester settlement; then he stops to consider for a minute.

> That carpenter is much on my mind:
> I think he was the first Maximus

> Anyhow, he was the first to make things,
> not just live off nature

and he partly opens the texture of the poem enough to let some of his own involvements become clearer.

      And he displays,
      in the record, some of those traits
      goes with that difference, traits present circumstances
      keep my eye on

                    for example, necessities the practise of the self,
                    that matter, that wood

the self, the growth, concern of the self is central to the figure
of Maximus.

   Still, even when the poem's broadest outlines are clear,
still there are snags. In the next lines

      Commerce with you, any of you who have tried to bend,
      any of you,
      not just the old few who wore beards,
      and culture - or the clean-shaven, the condottiere

there seems to be the implication that all someone like his
carpenter can have with the clean-shaven - is commerce.
Condottiere has sometimes the meaning of bandit, but it
can also mean the leader of a free band of mercenaries or
sometimes simply an adventurer. But not someone like a
Hartley, or a carpenter. Olson, like almost all of the poets in
the American idealistic tradition, does not consider trades-
men and the craftsmen as important to the society as artists.
The next four lines are an aside from the reference to the
older period of condottiere,

      (if I let any of that time in
      it is Verrocchio's cracked wood
      of Lorenzo, with a head like a Minnesota back
      or any worked schooner

and clear enough. The Minnesota back is probably Nagurski.
But the next five lines drift off again. Sometimes Olson is
like a small town talker who doesn't have to worry about
his audience; so he doesn't bother to explain himself as he
goes along.

                                        Charles Olson   29

> "Why did you give him a black hat,
> and a brim?" she queried,
> "when he wore tennis shoes,
> and held his pants up
> with a rope?"

Who gave who a black hat? Who is the woman? He never says. But, again like a small town talker, something always reminds him of something else, and he usually gets back to the point, even if it takes a lifetime of writing poetry to do it. Whoever got the black hat, he reminds Olson of Al Gorman (6 lines) who also held his pants up with a rope and cadged fish from incoming boats and left a fortune of $60,000. And Al Gorman reminds him of Mason Andrews (9 lines) who sold cat-nip, shoelaces, oranges, and gum that he carried around in a basket. And both of them, like the carpenter, or like Hartley, are an essence, a piece of what he's trying to say about the necessity of keeping the self together.

> How much the cracks matter, or seams in a ship, the absolutes
> of swelling . . .

> No where in man is there room for carelessnesses
> Or those arrogations I gave him the costume of

He slowly is returning to Hartley. The poem's second section opens,

> (As hands are put to the eyes' command

Hartley's hands and eyes, Olson seems to begin talking about something else,

> There is this rock breaches
> the earth: the Whale's Jaw
> my father stood inside of

but there is a Hartley painting of the whale's jaw, and he's already thinking about it, even though he has begun, obliquely, with a reference to his father with the same jaw.

>   I have a photograph, him
>   a smiling Jonah, forcing back those teeth
>   Or more Jehovah, he looks that strong
>   he could have split the rock
>   as it is split, and not
>   as Marsden Hartley painted it
>   so it's a canvas glove

The glove will return, as even Olson has to allow himself some point where the imagination can work. Hartley's rock looks like a canvas glove, and gloves, to Olson, have the inference of work, of working.

>   (such gloves
>   as fish-handlers - as Olsen, say,
>   or gardeners wear - or Ferrini ought to,
>   handling trash:
>
>   a man's hands,
>   as his eyes,
>   can get sores)

(The Olsen that he mentions was a drunken fishing boat captain who now carts fish - and has turned up in earlier letters. Ferrini, sad Ferrini, was living in Gloucester at the time and published one of the Letters in a local literary magazine. Something he did made Olson angry and Letter 5 will follow him for the rest of his days.)
But gloves - he develops the image of the glove in a reference to some of Hartley's best known paintings from this period.

>   such cloth he turned all things to,
>   made palms of hands of gulls,
>   Maine monoliths apostles,
>   a meal of fish a final supper
>   - made Crane a Marseilles matelot

His reference to their quality of imaginative vision. These paintings were the most intensely human of all of Hartley's work, and the figures of the fishermen, even of the gulls,

Charles Olson 31

were suffused with a sense of complete inner fulfillment. Olson, after describing them, suddenly pulls himself up short.

> Such transubstantiations
>
> as I am not permitted.

In his prose - his essays and critical writing - he has always said that the object *is*, "The inertial structure of the world is a real thing which not only exerts effects upon matter but in turn suffers such effects." From "Equal, That Is, To The Real Itself." And if something *is* then its structure is a finite entity which has its own dimension and space, and it has to be handled carefully in something as loose as poetic metaphor. It's as though imagination isn't to be trusted, and its uses should be limited. Olson's poetry has never been difficult in its imaginative image, only in its elisions and references. So difficult in these, that he could have been - often -uncomfortably trying to conceal the ordinariness of his materials by making the form of their presentation unnecessarily obscure. There is another implication, in the rejection of the imagination, that he makes more clearly in the Letter. It is the vague feeling that there is a weakness, a softness, in the loose drift of the imagination. Olson, almost in passing, becomes an artisan, a "worker," uneasy with the "humanness" of the imaginative vision.

> Such transubstantiations
>
> as I am not permitted,
> nor my father,
> who'd never have turned the Whale Jaw back
> to such humanness neither he nor I, as workers,
> are infatuated with

In his self-identification as worker some of the most complicated layers in the Letters become clearer. Not completely clear; since Olson is always difficult and challenging, but less opaque. His uneasiness with the imaginative vision has some of the gruffness of the New England countryman. As a poet he is also still the Charles Olson who was a fisherman, a carpenter, and postman. In this aspect of Olson is some of the poetry's brilliance, difficulty, insistence, and uniqueness.

As he begins to sort out the threads of the poem to bring it to a close - sorting out net lines before heaving them up - he returns to the point where he started, to Marsden Hartley, and Hartley's being within the self.

> What Hartley did was done according to his lights

and this accords with his Gloucester.

> The men of the matter of this city . . .
> are never
> doctrinaires

And having made his point Olson allows himself to reminisce, to think back to Hartley in Gloucester in the 1930's. With everything else in the Letters it becomes involved with something he remembers from the sea. The endless circling, eddying movement of the Letters, from the sea and its fishermen to Olson, his life, his conception of place and history, and this returning him to the sea, to Gloucester, to its people.

> (I only knew one such other other pair of hands as Hartley's
> Jake, his name
> was, mate aboard the Lafond's gill-netters.
> When I knew him his nails
> were all gone, peeled away from the brine they'd been in all
> the days of
> his life

There was something about Hartley's hands, just as there

was something in his eyes. The hands were thick and clumsy, and they seemed to have little relationship to his work as an artist - except that the work was thick and heavy and strong, even in his first work as painter of New England landscapes. Even more than in the first parts of the poem Olson has become the small town talker stringing together anecdotes. Perhaps it is anecdote that he has finally settled on to carry the structure of the poems. In the slow drifting reminiscences of older seamen and sunk boats and winter storms - even in the long recitations of local places and history - the pattern is of the casual anecdote, something suggesting something else. When the talker is an artisan, as Olson in these poems is an artisan, the handworker, the carpenter, the anecdotes have their own inner intensity, and their flow from one to another an expression of a larger emotional concern. The glimpse that Olson gives of Hartley does have its inner intensity. Is it only for someone who knows the paintings? Who is already familiar with Hartley's life? It could be. The response to anything in Maximus has to be personal. For someone already deeply familiar with the painter and his work Olson's poem, with all its rambling and discursion, is a sensitive, moving portrait. He was right to single out Hartley's eyes and hands - and to anticipate the last glance at Hartley's hands with the earlier image of the painted rock as canvas glove.

> Hartley's fingers gave this sense of soaking, the ends as
> > stubbed
> as Jake's, and each finger so thick and independent of the
> > other, his own
> hands were like gloves.
> > But not cloth. They stayed such rock
> > salt as Jake's
> were . . .

If the last reference, to Hartley's homosexuality, could be considered too sudden, too melodramatic, it was a central fact of Hartley's life, and his inability to resolve its tensions one of his life's tragedies. And certainly, used as an anecdote, it has its own inner force.

> As Jake's did,
> from baiting hooks for sixty years,
> as Hartley's,
> refusing woman's flesh

The poem, too, has its own inner force, despite its moments of obscurity. If it doesn't open up every theme of the Letters, it leaves enough spread out for the poet to spend years developing their emotional and philosophic implications. It is this that Olson has done in the rest of the Maximus Letters. Whatever someone decides about the poem any American poet beginning to sort out his poetic background will have to find his own place in the Letters - to find his own place in the American vision of Charles Olson's Gloucester.

Jack Spicer

"Imaginary Elegies, I-IV"

I think Spicer would probably have begun somewhere else; he would have wanted someone reading him to begin at some other place in his poetry. The Elegies are early poems, the first three written when he was twenty-five, the last finished when he was thirty. They are hard, clear poems, but without some of the insistences of the later poems. There are even - for Spicer - moments of softness.

> Lucky for us there are visible things
> > like oceans
> Which are always around,
> Continuous; disciplined adjuncts
> To the moment of sight.

The image has a directness, a clarity that he more and more moved away from as his poetic style changed. The Elegies are open, as somebody leaves a room open. The window is left unlatched and you can climb over the sill, step onto the rug, and walk around. The things that concerned him are there on the walls, put up with thumb tacks, left out on a table, piled up on the floor beside a chair. The later poems became almost like note cards that he carried around in his pockets to show you, laughing all the time you read them, but these earlier poems can be entered, moved through. There's enough space to sit and look at the things still strewn around this room that Spicer's left behind.

His concern, in the Elegies, begins with the poem, with his own absorption in poetry itself.

> Poetry, almost blind like a camera
> Is alive in sight only for a second. Click,
> Snap goes the eyelid of the eye before movement
> Almost as the word happens.

The imagery? A metallic, brilliant, hard "click" of camera, of poem - then the image turns, broadens, reaches out a tentative hand.

> One would not choose to blink and go blind
> After the instant.

His concern is that the poem is momentary and insufficient, that it has to have something outside of the lens's click.

> One would not choose
> To see the continuous Platonic patterns of birds flying
> Long after the stream of birds had dropped or had nested.

He has to have the "cold eternals," but only for their

> support of
> What is absolutely temporary.
> But not so sweet.

If a poem only does this much - a momentary, still camera image - just this, without growth or life - do we even need it? Does Spicer need it? He is still questioning as the first Elegy closes.

> All
> My eye has seen or ever could have seen
> I love
> I love - The eyelid clicks
> I see
> Cold poetry
> At the edge of their image

Click, the hard, metallic figure of the poem as camera, the

objects of his love edged with its hard glare. A sudden irritation as he's forced against the poem's limitations.

> It is as if we conjure the dead and they speak only
> Through our damned trumpets, through our damned
> > medium

Is the "damn" meant as a curse on poetry, on language? Or is it just an expression of his damned irritation? (Reading the line aloud it's still difficult to insist on one or the other.) But poetry is being considered and found inadequate.

II

"sur-re'al-ism, n. (F. surrealisme) Art. A modern movement in art and literature, influenced by Freudianism, purporting to express the subconscious mental activities by presenting images without order or sequence, as in a dream." The method of the surrealists can be useful, the juxtaposition of unrelated images, the discontinuity of thought and language, even if there is no real use of the subconscious. The trappings of surrealism have become almost an affectation of the New York school of poets, but in the work of these poets, as with Spicer, there is usually a conscious shaping and directing of the poem's larger movement, despite discontinuities in the poem surface. Often groups of lines, sections of Spicer's poems, seem to have this kind of unstructured form "presenting images without order or sequence," and in his juxtaposition of images without a clear interrelationship he forces the mind to consider new conceptual directions in the structure of the poem. Surrealism, as it breaks up the sense of movement within the poem, could be considered even anti-poetic, but in his questioning of poetry Spicer still moves as a poet. He uses the method - the sound - of surrealism - the limitless tying together of unlikes that is implicit in surrealist technique - but in the larger outlines of the poem he is still thinking through image to idea. The materials of the poem seem to come from the subconscious, but the structuring of the materials is done by a conscious poetic intelligence.

> God must have a big eye to see everything
> That we have lost or forgotten.

As he begins again the eye of the camera, the instant of the poem, is reiterated with the "see" of God, and the dead speaking only through the damned trumpets have become part of the "everything" that we have lost or forgotten. Then with a subtle shifting the eye of God becomes the moon.

> The moon is God's big yellow eye remembering
> What we have lost or never thought,

A pulling together, a tying of thought to thought, of image to image. The "lost" now can include the "never thought."

> That's why
> The moon looks raw and ghostly in the dark,

The poetry moves in sudden leaps of association. The moon has seen - "is" - "the objects that we never saw." There is the overhanging sense of the surrealistic, but it is never forced. It is almost an intellectual use of the technique, with strong differences between his imagery and the imagery of a Rimbaud. Rimbaud's intensity comes from the senses, from the touch, feel, color, scene - even in his use of the discontinuous there is an opulence of the senses that Gautier would have responded to, a breathing in at the nostrils of smells, tastes, sensations.

"Une matinée couverte, en juillet. Un goût de cendres vole dans l'air; - une odeur de bois suant dans l'âtre - les fleurs rouies - le saccage des promenades, - la bruine des canaux par les champs, - pourquoi pas déjà les joujoux et l'encens?"

"An overcast morning, in July. A taste of ashes flies

through the air; - an odor of wood sweating on the hearth, - dew - wet flowers - devastation along the promenades - the mist of the canals over the fields - why not already toys and incense ?"

Incense and toys - so little like the camera image of Spicer's first elegy, but Spicer wrote, later, "A Fake Novel About The Life Of Arthur Rimbaud," and the affinity seems to be conscious on Spicer's part. Spicer's surrealism is of the mind, not of the senses, the pragmatic American use of a technique, rather than giving way to its full implications. In its seeming lack of coherence Spicer's mind moves along the streams of light that an image throws.

> Tarot cards
> Make love to other Tarot cards. Here agony
> Is just imagination's sister bitch.
> This is the sun-tormented castle which
> Reflects the sun. Da dada da.
> The castle sings.
> Da. I don't remember what I lost. Dada.

(Dada? - humming a song? suggesting childhood? referring to Dadaism? It seems to be all three.) And it's almost as though the poem interrupted him. The castle sings, but distantly, obliquely. The poem, despite his protest at its limitations, has become more than the instant of camera image. He has stepped beyond the image into the poem itself, the thought completely directed from an inner intensity. Whatever objections he raised to poetry in his opening lines he has resolved them. The poem does more than just record the instant, by its act of discontinuity it somehow takes on its own inner dimension, and he lets the poem flow into this new direction, into a new shape and a new tension.

> But look now, in this room, see the moon-children
> Wolf, bear, and other, dragon, dove.
> Look now, in this room, see the moon-children
> Flying, crawling, swimming, burning

Vacant with beauty
Hear them whisper.

III

Always an anticipation of a poem's movements, the mind
going beyond it to try to follow the line even before the line
is spoken. There is a suggestion of resonance in the antici-
pated turning of sound - and Spicer's third elegy grows
from the directions of the earlier two. The poem's image has
moved only a few steps from his conception of the moon as
God's eye, from the camera to the eye of God remembering
what we lost or never thought, reaching further as a poem
reaches, without dropping anything that it has once held.
A stone is dropped and water spills - then subsides. The
movements a poem makes are silent in their unending movement. From the moon the image shifts to the sun - but the
moon still lingers in the sky, and implicit in the sun is the
moon, is the eye of the camera. The sun swells beyond their
dimensions but contains them both, as Spicer contains all
three.

> God's other eye is good and gold. So bright
> The sunblinds. His eye is accurate His eye
> observes the goodness of the light it shines
> Then, pouncing like a cat devours
> Each golden trace of light
> It saw and shined.
> Cat feeds on mouse. God feeds on God. God's goodness is
> A black and blinding cannibal with sunny teeth
> That only eats itself.

And out of the distant intellect of the poem a sudden sense
of pain. It is this moment that clarifies the place of the poet
in the Elegies, that makes them a point to begin with Spicer.
When he felt this pain in the later poems he usually laughed,
and the laughter became a bitter hedge around the limits of
his emotions. Even in this early poem he seems to feel that

he's gone too far, that he has to get back to the distance of the first sections. In an abrupt, almost Eliot-like shift - the Eliot of "Hurry up, please, it's time" or the first uncomfortable phrasings of the Quartets - he makes a tentative move toward the less painful of the poem's selves, toward the innocent figures of the final lines of the second elegy.

> There is an innocent old sun quite cold in cloud.
> The ache of sunshine stops.
> God is gone God is gone.
> Nothing was quite as good.
> It's getting late. Put on your coat.
> It's getting dark. It's getting cold.

And the poem draws within itself for a still moment of reflection.

> Most things happen in twilight
> When the sun goes down and the moon hasn't come
> And the earth dances.
> Most things happen in twilight
> When neither eye is open
> And the earth dances.

But a momentary reflection is not movement, only a cessation of movement. The poem still hangs in the sun's heat and he allows the image to crowd in on him again. The poem's point of deepest intensity? He is using all of the poet's resources to move the poem into a deepening imagery of sun and heat and bodies, without thought, without hesitation, without defense.

> The boys above the swimming pool receive the sun.
> Their groins are pressed against the warm cement.
> They look as if they dream. As if their bodies dream.
> Rescue their bodies from the poisoned sun
> Shelter the dreamers. They're like lobsters now
> Hot red and private as they dream.

He is at the slow point of breath when the poem's meaning is a grouping of sensations beyond the hand's reach. In the afternoon sun fingers touch the skin, but what is the expression of the face? Spicer has turned to stare at himself as a poet, to find what his hands can reach out to.

> Unbind the dreamers.
>   Poet,
> Be like God.

IV

Did five years really go by between the first three elegies and the fourth? Spicer suggests it.

> Yes, be like God. I wonder what I thought
> When I wrote that. The dreamers sag a bit.
> As if five years had thickened on their flesh
> Or on my eyes.

There is a sudden return of the anger of the sun image,

> Should I throw rocks at them
> To make their naked private bodies bleed?

But it passes as quickly as it came.

> No Let them sleep.

Too much has gone by, too much has happened, the time to be angry has passed. The tone becomes elegiac, the murmur of the poem's sound finally becoming the elegy of the title.

> This much I've learned
> In these five years in what I spent and earned:
> Time does not finish a poem.

The imagery is still of oceans, suns, moons, but they are taken from a different view point.

> The dummies in the empty fun house watch
> The tides wash in and out. The thick old moon
> Shines through the rotten timbers every night.

Spicer has left the barrenness of his camera eye and the poem broadens, drifts under the heavy sun, its streaming surface glistening and yellow, heavy enough to sustain his weight. He drifts with it.

> This much I've learned
> In these five years in what I've spent and earned:
> That two-eyed monster God is still above.
> I saw him once when I was young and once
> When I was seized with madness, or was I seized
> and mad because I saw him once.

He has drifted so far from his questioning of the poem, of poetry, from the suggestion, hint of cruelty or anger or distrust as each section began. From his rejection of poetry as anything beyond the coldness of an image. How could he, as a poet, dull his own weapons? The distance of his poetry persists, the distance between sense and image - it is only through his mind, his conscious thought, that the image enters his being - but once it has entered him it draws from him for its own strength, its own vitality, and he lets it live within him. For the poem lives, has its own life. If he at first persisted,

> One would not choose
> To see the continuous Platonic pattern of birds flying
> Long after the stream of birds has dropped or nested.

he no longer persists. The Elegies, which began as a questioning of poetry, end as an acceptance. In their sudden moments of openness they have yielded a glimpse of Spicer, and the glimpse is of a man who was a poet.

> Above the giant funhouses and the ghosts
> I hear the seagulls call. They're going west
> Toward some great Cataline of a dream
> Out where the poem ends.
> But does it end?
> The birds are still in flight. Believe the birds.

Robert Duncan

"Lammas Dream Poem"

Duncan, in so many ways, does battle for us all. His battle
for poetry and for the experience of the poem is so determined
and so persistent that anyone involved with poetry in the
United States today is in his debt. It is a period when poetry
has little weight in the society's clumsy scales. Even the poets
who are read don't tip balances or shift allegiances. Duncan,
through all of this, persists, writes, publishes, talks, creates;
bringing to everything in his work the same sense of the
beauty and the relevance of the poetic experience. I don't
mean by this that I respond as fully to all of the poetry, as
fully to every dimension of his poetics, but for a moment I
want to separate the poet and his work and give to Duncan
the fullest measuring of his role as poet and artist. It is par-
ticularly difficult for a poet like Duncan because he is writing
at a time when the aesthetic of the poem has already come to
emotional terms with the loss of the audience. The response
of the contemporary poet has been to decide that the reaction
of the reader is of no importance to the experience of the
poem. Everyone still goes on with the late 19th century ideal
of art for art's sake. Within England's class structure, where
the poet had to toady or leave, this may have had some kind
of reality, but it has forced American poetry away from the
strengthening that comes from reader's response, away from
the toughening of line and phrase that comes from letting
the poem push its way through a crowd. Instead of the fierce

commitment of the Soviet poets or the passion of the great Spanish group of the Generation of 1927 the American and English poet is left with a concept of the poem that refuses to go beyond the limits of the poet's person in its forms and its judgments.

Duncan is not responsible for the contemporary aesthetic of the poem and his work often does break through the sour limitings that surround the modern poem. It is necessary to write as though the audience were there, or there won't ever be an audience for poetry. In his weakest poems Duncan does seem to be hemmed in, and the emotion comes almost entirely from the sense of writing poetry. The excitement is in the creating of the poem, a secondary emotion, rather than a primary emotional response to the reality of experience. But this is also involved with his excitement with the role of the poet and in this is perhaps his central strength. He persists, he goes on, and the work is shaped and directed by his fervent belief in the poem as a creative force. Sometimes the poetry is overly allusive, overly elaborate, the levels of reference so tenuous that the poem loses emotional directness; but when he does place himself in the poem, when it becomes clearly an expression of himself as human being rather than himself as poet - as in "Lammas Dream Poem" - then the fabric of language and reference becomes an intense revelation of the poetic experience.

The title has been changed - to "My Mother Would Be A Falconress" in its collected version - but I think he has lost some of the symbolism that was in the title "Lammas Dream Poem." Lammas? - Anglo-Saxon, from hlammesse, hlaf-maesse, the loaf Mass, bread feast. Hlaf - loaf, maesse - Mass. The first day of August, Lammas Day, or the time of year. Duncan, in an introduction, " . . . And when I wrote down the hour and date, I saw it was Lammas. 'August 1, 1964,' I wrote: 'Lammas tide, 2 A.M.' " Lammas tide - around Lammas Day. The poem has no involvement with Lammas, but its symbolism is involved with the medieval sport of falconry and the word Lammas has an association with the medieval, with the conception of the year in ceremonies and functions.

> My mother would be a falconress
> And I, her gay falcon treading her wrist,
> would fly to bring back
> from the blue of the sky to her, bleeding, a prize

The medieval pageantry of the falcon, of falconry, as a complex image of his relationship with his mother. It has a distant unreality, but with its entangling image of mother-son, falconress -falcon, an immediate emotional insistence. The cry is heard within us, but from - medieval, richly ornate - a complex involvement of past. A dream of poem image, a wakening within poem image. Duncan,". . . I had awakend at two in the night with the lines repeated insistently in my mind." The immediacy of the phrase held the poem's image within it, the whole of the poem implicit in its directions.

What is a falcon concerned with? With his captivity? his captor? his prey? Who knows about falcons? Duncan's falcon has so little to do with the ferocity of the hunting falcon. His falcon has become a child, while still a bird of prey tied to a wrist.

> I dream in my little hood with many bells
> jangling when I'd turn my head

and, childlike, its involvement is with its captor.

> she sends me as far as her will goes.
> She lets me ride to the end of her curb
> where I fall back in anguish.
> I dread that she will cast me away,
> for I fall, I mis-take, I fail in her mission.

How can Duncan achieve an image of such complex physical involvement? To make himself the hawk and the hawk himself. The image has its own strength, and the brilliance of the art - the unity of the language - sustains it. There is something in the image of the son as a young hawk on his mother's wrist - lean, impatient, savage - treading the wrist waiting for the hood to be untied from its eyes - an imagination's vision of the mother-son relationship that opens and extends the reality of that relationship.

The poem moves on as the image shifts, moves from its first subtle implications to its widest circumference of meaning, and it grows as his consciousness of the image grows. At the opening of the poem he places its emphasis on the structured ritual of medieval hawking, but with himself identified as the hawk still tied to the falconer's wrist, himself as the child who must rise from the close fettering of the falconress who has bound him.

> For she has muffled my dreams in the hood she has made me,
> sewn round with bells, jangling when I move
> She uses a barb that brings me to cower.

Even in his brief moments of flight - in the soaring spiral of the hawk as it hunts - it isn't the prey, but still his captor who absorbs him.

> She sends me abroad to try my wings
> and I come back to her. I would bring down
> the little birds to her
> I may not tear into, I must bring back perfectly.

It is a poem of desperations, of desperate love and as desperate sadness. He must tear himself free, but he will always be entangled in their relationship.

> Yet it would have been beautiful, if she had carried me,
> always, in a little hood with the bells ringing,
> at her wrist, and her riding
> to the great falcon hunt, and me
> flying up to the curb of my heart from her heart

to bring down the skylark from the blue to her feet,
straining, and then released for the flight.

He has bared them and left them to the implications of
their relationship as mother and son.

In the elaborations of his themes, in his responses to his
experience Duncan often seems to me to be misplaced - to be
out of his time. The sense of the medieval is strongly figured
in his work. It isn't the early medieval temper that interests
him - the hammered iron of immaculate conception, Virgin
birth, and divine resurrection - as much as it is the point of
medieval thought when the first fascinations of the renaissance, the myths of Greece and Rome, the paganism of the
earth and sky, had begun to leaven the ferocity of medieval
Christianity. He isn't involved in the complex of ideas that
determined the mood of the period; he isn't committed either
to a cult of Aphrodite or to the suppression of Aphrodite.
The threads of medieval and renaissance thought are woven
through his work with equal strength and color. Instead, in
his fascination with the terms and garments and names and
objects of the medieval period he seems to be closer in attitude to the 19th Century Pre-Raphaelite Brotherhood. In
many of the poems I feel the same emotional response that I
have in front of a Burne-Jones painting, or in the work of
Holman Hunt or the Rossettis, in the Joan of Arcs, the vi-
sions of Beatrice, the legends of the Grail. In poems that describe his own approach to writing the mood is the same kind
of rich daydream that the Pre-Raphaelites painted.
From Passages 2.

            my mind a shuttle among
                    set strings of the music
        lets a weft of dream grow in the day time,
                    an increment of associations,
            luminous soft threads,
        the thrown glamour, crossing and recrossing,

the twisted sinews underlying the work.

Back of the images, the few cords that bind
    meaning in the word-flow,
            the rivering web
        rises among wit and senses
    gathering the wool into its full cloth.

Perhaps because of this deep responsiveness Duncan has the widest range of concerns and fascinations of all his contemporaries. In some of the Passages there is the Poundian heaviness of encyclopedic reading summaries, but when he became immersed in the Cantos Pound virtually gave up writing anything else. Duncan began the Passages when he was already fully formed as a poet, and they have continued to express his fullest range of subject. The Passages have even opened out into bitter denunciation of America's war in Vietnam. From Passages 26,

against the bloody verse America writes over Asia

we must recall   to hold   by property rights that

are not private (individual) or public rights but

given properties of our common humanity.

The Passages alternate with sections from his other extended poem, The Structure of Rime, and he also continues writing short poems as diverse as his translations from Nerval or "The Christ In The Olive Grove." He even involves himself in other poets so deeply that he reflects their style in his own poems derived from them. There was the long series of pieces stemming from Gertrude Stein, the responses to H.D. and Zukofsky, the suggestions of Pound in the Passages. The poems are as contemporary in subject as the defense of the student demonstrators in Passages 21, as long reaching as "This Place Rumord To Have Been Sodom." But despite the concern for the present, the searching for theme in the present, it would still be difficult to call him a modern poet. The things that most characterize modern poetry aren't present in his work. He isn't deeply concerned with the image. He is concerned with imagery, but not with imagism. He describes, but he doesn't have the kind of visual realizations that Williams or Creeley or even Olson have. The rhythm of the poetry also has no sense of the breath's measure or limitation. Often the poems have been assembled from groups of notes and their different cadences make it impossible to find a breath rhythm that lies through all of them. It is poetry without a place. Lacking the sentimentality of the 19th Century, the order and precision of the 18th, the religious passion or courtly posturing of the 17th, it has to go back to this point where the medieval and the renaissance mingle,where everything is suddenly being picked up and looked at anew, and for the first time in so many centuries there is no boundary to what can be considered. This is the sense of the ornateness as he fills his poems with objects and attitudes; the reach of the work as he leans out to gather what he can into the image and the idea. He has been displaced, and he has to struggle again and again to find his place anew.

In the Lammas poem the struggle is more direct, more immediate. It is his struggle to grow beyond the limits of a first self, and the violence leaves its marks on him. He finally springs from the wrist in a great, soaring upward flight.

> Ah, but high, high in the air I flew.
> And far, far beyond the curb of her will,
> were the blue hills where the falcons nest,
> and then I saw west to the dying sun,
> It seemed my human soul went down in flames. . .
>
> far, far beyond the curb of her will
> to horizons of stars beyond the ringing hills of the world
>   where the falcons nest

Robert Duncan 53

I saw, and I tore at her wrist with my savage beak.
I flew, as if sight flew from the anguish in her eyes beyond
    her sight,
sent my striking loose, from the cruel strike at her wrist,
striking out from the blood to be free of her.

A momentary implication beyond the poem? "the blue hills where the falcons nest . . ." " . . . the ringing hills of the world where the falcons nest." A glorying in the falcon? A glorying in something more than the growth from childhood to manhood that is involved with the tearing free from his mother's wrist? Beyond the immediate image could there be another level of image within the vision of the falcon, the poem becoming an allegory of his struggle with his mother as he reached toward his homosexual being, "the blue hills where the falcons nest?" For a moment the poem looks beyond the struggle between the falconer and the falcon, instead of his absorption with his captor he suddenly turns and looks toward something definite and direct, romantic in its glimpse of " . . . horizons of stars . . ."

But the poem's direction hasn't shifted. The movement has given a subtle undertone to the poem's larger structure. The pulse of the poem is the son's effort to be free of his mother, and Duncan allows only a hint of anything beyond their blind struggle. The poem's involvement is most total on this level of image, and even the poem's ambiguities become part of its total reality. The poem Duncan has written is the poem image of a child's desperate yearning to be free. The poem's deepest tragedy is in the duality of maturity - that in the man, the child, in pain and torment, is still enclosed.

My mother would be a falconress,
and even now, years after this
when the wounds I left her had surely heald,
and the woman is dead,
her fierce eyes closed, and if her heart

were broken, it is stilld;
I would be a falcon and go free.
I tread her wrist and wear the hood,
talking to myself, and would draw blood.

Duncan could not have bared himself more fully. The poem's act of self acknowledgement could not be more complete.

Gary Snyder

"How To Make Stew In The Pinacate Desert
Recipe for Locke and Drum"

A poem of simplicities — of affecting simplicities - and I am
affected by it, as I am by Snyder - and I am uncertain about
it, as I am uncertain about Snyder. Not uncertain about his
effectiveness as a poet - Snyder is brilliant and unmistakeable
- but I am uncertain of the innocence that could write a poem
of the simplicity of "How To Make Stew In The Pinacate
Desert." It is an innocence that somehow has the feeling of
a stance, an attitude - which would make it not innocent -
but his poem, like Snyder, has the feeling of completeness,
that the poem, and he, is what it says it is. Within the poem
are larger implications, but it is - simply - a recipe for cooking
stew in the desert, written for some friends.

> A. J. Bayless market bent wire roller basket buy up parsnip,
>> onion
>> carrot, rutabaga and potatoes, bell green pepper
>> & nine cuts of dark beef shank.
>> They run there on their legs, that makes meat tasty.

Almost without art, without guile. The only suggestion
of something else in its simplicity is the implied excitement
in the movement of the first phrase. "A. J. Bayless market
bent wire roller basket . . ." instead of "Go to the A. J.
Bayless market . . ." The "bent wire roller basket" is an impression, a glimpse, an image of the market interior, not an
elision of "get a bent wire basket . . ." In his hurry, in his

excitement, only time for glimpses. But why excitement over cooking a stew? The simplicity is only an immediate face of the poem, an attitude that Snyder is using to direct the poem's movement. And it is a poem, even if it reads like a recipe.

> Seven at night in Tuscon, get some bisquick for the
> dumplings.
> Have some bacon. Go to Hadley's in the kitchen right
> beside the
> frying steak - Diana on the phone -

It is - also - more than a poem. In its simplicities and immediacies Snyder is describing a ceremony. The definiteness of the directions, the care of the details, for the vegetables, the meat, the times, places, spaces, all the movements of a ceremony. A simple ceremony, but by the act of ceremony itself the levels of meaning have become multiple, the steps of the ceremony followed with the image of their implied meanings. A ceremony for what, to yield what? Ceremonies have a circumference beyond their immediate event that gives even their confusions a larger importance. Even Gary Snyder's ceremony for making beef stew in the desert outside of Tucson, Arizona.

> . . . get a little plastic bag from
> Drum -
> Fill it up with tarragon and chili: four bay leaves; black
> pepper
> corns and basil; powdered oregano, something free, maybe
> about
> two teaspoons of salt.

Snyder's ceremony is like much of his poetry, an attempt to reenact the experience of the natural environment. *Walden* written in a small hand. An American ceremony, affirmed over and over by American writers who, like Snyder, have felt the necessity of continuing this experience. They've thought of it either as a step toward a "true" environment - a positive stance - or as a step away from the "false" environment of the American city - a negative stance. For Snyder the ceremony is a step toward, a positive movement and direction, its affirmation so self-evident that he doesn't even feel the necessity of justifying it. His poetry has had this same clarity of affirmation from his earliest books. *Rip Rap* has as little artifice as his recipe for stew. The poems - it was his first book - almost completely outlined the spaces that his poetry has filled since. The opening poem, "Mid-August at Sourdough Mountain Lookout," ends,

> I cannot remember things I once read
> A few friends, but they are in cities.
> Drinking cold snow-water from a tin cup
> Looking down for miles
> Through high still air.

Even in a book as early as *Rip Rap* the innocence was directly and clearly present.

His poetry has this openness, this simplicity, but it also has a fullness, a sense of completeness. Everything in the poems comes out of his involvement with the earth in its deepest sense. In *Rip Rap* there is the shamanism of "Praise for Sick Women," poems from his loose wandering as a merchant seaman, poems from his life in the mountains of the Pacific Northwest, from his life in Japan - the "great stone garden in the sea" — the themes that have continued through his poetry. In all of it is the same innocence - the same guarded distance from the concept of a city and a crowd. Snyder would have liked to live his life as part of a tribe, without a tribe he has had to develop his own rituals toward the earth and its creatures. The years he has spent in Zen studies in Japan could have emphasized the ceremonial in a poem about a desert stew - since so much of the life in a monastery is ceremonial - but it could as well come out of his feeling of the necessity of the tribe and its ritual.

But the poetry still has a confusing element, its certainty is sometimes disquieting. The simplicity, the innocence sometimes has an overtone of obviousness, of insistence. Does Snyder mean it? Is his innocence genuine, despite the obvious complexity of his attitude toward it? Within its small frame even a poem like the stew recipe is insisting on the uniqueness of the wilderness experience, its attitudes - through his own involved feeling of tribe and earth - rooted in the Rousseauist vision of the romantic primitive, and to its manifestation through the American philosophic ideal of an essential innocence in the wild and the untouched. A long lived plant with deep roots, a summer sumac with its branches cut away but still growing in its roots and forcing its green swatch of leaf into the afternoon's heat. Thoreau, ranging the same ground, would have stepped further, would have related the ceremony of cooking a desert stew to his own, and intensely personal, philosophy; but Thoreau, without being conscious of it, was less innocent than Snyder. From *Walden*,

> It is hard to provide and cook so simple and clean a diet as will not offend the imagination: but this, I think, is to be fed when we feed the body: they should both sit down at the same table. Yet perhaps this may be done. The fruits eaten temperately need not make us ashamed of our appetites, nor interrupt the worthiest pursuits. But put an extra condiment into your dish, and it will poison you. It is not worth the while to live by rich cookery. Most men would feel shame if caught preparing with their own hands precisely such a dinner, whether of animal or vegetable food, as is every day prepared for them by others. Yet till this is otherwise we are not civilized, and, if gentlemen and ladies, are not true men and women . . .

In a period when nearly everybody made stew in the woods Thoreau had to do more than list the ingredients and the kind of firewood. Snyder, at a time when very few people make stew in the desert, has only to describe the steps of his simple ceremony.

The innocence that is close to the center of the experience, the consciousness that moves Snyder's poem, is it a true innocence? It seems to have a still breath of naiveté, to be even less involved with the world at the farthest end of the railroad than Thoreau was at his pond. But Snyder's individuality has a complexity of depth and mood. He has come to it from a new conception, the concept of an innocence that builds itself through an awareness of what it has to avoid. A self-chosen innocence. Snyder has sensed that his response to much of what the American environment is forcing in on him has to be an act of rejection. His rejection is so complete that nothing of this response is even present in the poem. Nothing in his description of his stew making ceremony suggests that he is self-conscious - even self-aware that the simplicity of the poem, in itself, has to be an expression of his own complexity. The poem, for him, is as complete within itself as a piece of stone.

> Now down in Sonora, Pinacate country, build a fire of
> Ocotillo,
> broken twigs and bits of ironwood, in an open ring of lava:
> rake
> some coals aside (and if you're smart) to windward,
> keep the other half ablaze for heat and light.
> Set Drum's fourteen-inch dutch oven with three legs
> across the
> embers.

The care for detail, the insistence on detail, has the same kind of concentration as a paragraph on fire building in a Boy Scout manual - even to the advice about raking the coals aside to windward - and it is as isolated in its implications. There is no movement of thought away from the fire, only

Gary Snyder 61

movement around it. The fire, like the poem, is complete within itself. There aren't any adjectives, phrases, confusions to the simple act of building it. In its completeness, its lack of implication, it becomes an innocence so intensely felt that - as Snyder knew - it has no need of affirmation. In itself the ceremonial cooking of a stew in the desert is the assertion of innocence. The details become as bare, as sharply outlined in their clarity as the dried brushwood piled on the desert floor.

> Now put in the strips of bacon.
> In another pan have all the vegetables cleaned up and peeled and sliced . . .
> add the little bag of herbs - cook it all five minutes more - and then throw in the pan of all the rest.
> Cover it up with big hot lid all heavy, sit and wait, or drink budweiser beer.

Budweiser beer? Was that what he drank the first time? Does he have to do everything just as he did it the first time? Indian boys, playing, trail each other across the stones and through the dry brush with a trace of a heel or a still damp spot in a stream bed where a stone was kicked out of the way. Trailing behind to find the place where he has been before, Snyder's poem follows the marks left by bags of herbs, bits of ironwood, and cans of Budweiser beer. It is a place where other American poets have spent long years of their lives - in the dream of wilderness experience — of the relationship of the land and the trees, the sky and earth. To be there, at that place, is enough, without need of description, or perhaps can't be described. At least not by Snyder, whose innocence is complete. An innocence that knows, but denies its knowledge. The moral implication is tangled and obscure, a denial of knowledge as a form of innocence, but he would probably refuse even to consider the implication. It could be that at this place in the American journey it is the only innocence left to us.

> And let it cook ten minutes more
> And lift the black pot off the fire
> to set aside another good ten minutes.

As description the poem catches some of the excitement of fending for food and warmth in the desert night - the "black pot"- blackened by the smoky sticks used for firewood - the time sitting and waiting for the pot to cool. And there is no question for him of the reality of the experience - or in the reality of the innocence of which the experience is an expression. The poem ends in the stillness of the dwindling fire and the smell of wood smoke in the night air.

> Dish it up and eat it with a spoon, sitting on a poncho in the dark.

The dishes still have to be washed - or at least some water rinsed in the pot so it won't be too hard to clean in the morning - and the fire banked in for the night, but with the stew gone Snyder's small ceremony is over.

Lew Welch

"Chicago Poem"

> I lived here . . .

(Welch's "here" is Chicago)

> I lived here 5 years before I could
>   meet the middle western day with anything approaching
> Dignity. It's a place that lets you
>   understand why the Bible is the way it is:
> Proud people cannot live here.

The American innocent - Lew Welch, as well as Gary Snyder. The American idealist, the American Adam, still unable to accept the reality of the city. Snyder has already left it. He's beyond even any considering of the city or its people. Welch, his "Chicago Poem," is still in it - but only long enough to look around a last time before he leaves to follow Snyder into the woods, back into the imagined dream of the American wilderness.

In his poem it's almost as though Welch were standing on a street corner with his arms folded, trying to tell somebody what he thinks about Chicago. The language is casual, immediate, direct. He's only concerned with telling you what's on his mind, half listening to whatever anybody else is saying. The poem is mostly his side of the conversation. He is angry about Chicago, he is angry about the city, but he doesn't think he can do anything to change it; so there isn't a reformer's hard shrillness in the poem. Instead there's a fierce sense of self-preservation. It is the city, as a social or-

ganism; Chicago, as the specific city, that he has to get out
of. He began with the center of the city - he moves on to
the mills below the south side.

> The land's too flat. Ugly sullen and big . . .

> In the mills and refineries of its south side Chicago
> passes its natural gas in flames
> Bouncing like bunsens from stacks a hundred feet high.
> The stench stabs at your eyeballs.
> The whole sky green and yellow backdrop for the skeleton
> steel of a bombed-out town.

Looking at the ugliness of south Chicago he has changed his
tone - he's stopped being casual. Instead of a street corner
conversation there's an abrupt metaphor of body smells, ". . .
passes its natural gas in flames. . ." and destruction, ". . .the
whole sky . . . backdrop for the skeleton steel of a bombed-
out town." Even when someone just tries to preserve a part
of himself the city forces his voice to become a little harder,
the tone a little more strident. As Welch looks at the dirt and
the clutter around his street corner he finds it harder to talk
easily. He has his own resentments. American poetry hadn't
idealized the city, but it sometimes has idealized the indus-
trial process that produced the city - the workers, the jobs,
the sweating and the effort of the building of the city. Welch
is as resentful of this idealization as he is of the city itself.

> Remember the movies in grammar school? The goggled men
> doing strong things in
> Showers of steel sparks? . . .
> Blast of orange like a sunset? Or an orange?

He denies the idealization, denies the beauty. He doesn't
even allow the idealization to the people who thought they
found beauty in it.

> It was photographed by a fairy, thrilled as a girl, or
> a Nazi who wished there were people
> Behind that door . . .

The city has to be fled from - the innocence, the unity of
the self kept whole. Keep your hands in your pockets so nobody can steal your carfare, stand with your back against
the wall so nobody can get in behind you. But who wants to
believe that the city's that bad? Who wants to think that he
has to keep his door locked if he goes downstairs to get the
mail, or that he has to wear shoes he doesn't care about if he
wants to sleep in the park. So you try to think - at least for
a while - that the city's possible, but there are just too many
people - too many faces, hands, mouths - for you to do anything but distrust each other. And the distrust - since there
was at first an effort to trust - becomes disillusion - who
thought it could be anything - who thought that there was
a place, a breath of life in the city.

> It was 5 years until I could afford to recognize the ferocity,
> and when the movement outside the door has a low, hostile
> sound you have to find a refuge.
> Then I put some
> Love into my house. Finally I found some quiet
> and a farm where they let me shoot pheasant.

Even the violent act of killing - shooting birds - for
Welch becomes a refuge from the city's impersonal violence.
His romantic innocence is less coherent than Gary Snyder's
intellectual innocence and he is able to kill without thinking
of anything beyond his relationship to the raw world of the
air and the lake and a dying fish.

> Standing in the boat one night I watched the lake go
> absolutely
> flat. Smaller than raindrops, and only
> Here and there, the feeding rings of fish were visible 100
> yards
> away - and the Blue Gill caught that afternoon
> Lifted from its northern lake like a tropical! Jewel at its ear.
> Belly gold so bright you'd swear he had a
> Light in there. His color faded with his life. A small
> green fish.

Lew Welch 67

Even the act of death is innocent - if it is a death of person against person, not a city death. So you get out into the woods, out in a boat in the lake. Even hunting becomes an expression of a different self. The city denies the self, stifles the self so the poet flees the city to keep something - some innocence - of the self. The American romantic, a poet like Welch, insists that the city is the evil being.

> All things considered, it's a gentle and an undemanding
>   planet, even here. Far gentler
> Here than any of a dozen other places. The trouble is
>   always and only with what we build on top of it.

In another society, more conscious of its own organism, of its own interrelationships, this leads to revolutions. Get out in the streets, shout at people, get them to change the city, make the streets come alive, the city a place for the innocent idealist. But with the trees always just beyond the fringe of the fields the American romantic has usually just walked a-way, taken his tent out into the wilderness, built his cabin beside a pond. The land itself is too gentle to distrust.

> There's nobody to blame. You can't fix it and you
>   can't make it go away. It does no good appealing
> To some ill-invented Thunderer
>   brooding above some unimaginable crag . . .

So you can't blame, can't organize, can't change. Just stand around on the street corner and look uncomfortably over your shoulder - not letting the city get too close. If everybody still lived in small towns and you could get out along the river to fish, and you could go off into the woods - even go lie on your back in a field and listen to the train whistle past. But you can't do anything about the city. An innocence of idealism, an indulgence of idealism - but not too much else the poet can do about his situation. The small town never decided what to do with poets, the cities listen even less; so the poet is left to shift for himself.

> Driving back I saw Chicago rising in its gases and I
> knew again that never will the
> Man be made to stand against this pitiless, unparalleled
> monstrosity.

Finally Welch is forced to drop his attitude of disengagement, take his hands out of his pockets to gesture. The language becomes a flat, insistent reflection of his anger at the city's unrelenting ugliness.

> . . . It
> Snuffles on the beach of its Great Lake like a
> blind, red rhinocerous.

But the romantic idealist involves himself - gives himself - and even in his anger Welch still has to pull himself away from the city. He has to get away - will get away - but knowing that he leaves a dimension of his life in it. He is able to leave it, because of his idealism. He is too disappointed to try to do anything about the city. To do anything more than stand and look around at its ugliness. Stand on the street corner with his hands stuffed back in his pockets and stare unhappily around him at the painted board fences and the dirty brick walls. He knows - must know - that he doesn't have an alternative in the fields hunting, or sleeping in the woods - but the American poet, the romantic innocent, has to believe that he might have this alternative, and even if he does not have it, that it's still the ideal for him to look for.

> You can't fix it. You can't make it go away.
> I don't know what you're going to do about it,
> But I know what I'm going to do about it. I'm just
> going to walk away from it. Maybe
> A small part of it will die if I'm not around
>
> feeding it anymore.

He stands on his street corner talking a little loudly to be heard over the traffic noise, and the people standing around him slowly nod, agreeing.

Lew Welch 69

Allen Ginsberg

"American Change"

To begin reading Ginsberg is just to find a place and begin - pick a page and read it - since it's all a single poem, as Whitman is a single poem, as Hart Crane tried to be a single poem. I don't know even if "poem" is the word for Ginsberg's long crying voice. The poem, in its singleness, is his life - as Whitman's was only in part his life. Whatever else we have of Ginsberg we have *him*. The opening line of "Howl," "I saw the best minds of my generation destroyed by madness" is as much confessional as the most painful self revelation of "Kaddish." So - a poem, to begin, to place, to find. "American Change." In its abrupt excitement a sudden opening of insight, its imagery a new approach to some of his central themes. It is improvisatory, as all his poetry is improvisatory, but the form, vocabulary, rhythm is already implicit in his life - there is a coherence that is identifiable. "American Change" doesn't reach for as much as some of the longer pieces of his poem, but it reaches for the same things and it has a definiteness that other pieces haven't always had. The concepts of "better" - the artistic sense of "good" - don't have any meaning for Ginsberg. But definiteness does have a reality he might accept. When asked if he thinks a poem is "good," Ginsberg always answers, "What do you mean by good?"

The same themes, the same attitudes, and the assumptions that all of the poets around Ginsberg share - the intense idealism, the social naivete, the centering on the lyric of the self, the use of familiar linguistic materials - all of this is expressive of Ginsberg's concerns. His own definiteness as poet is a verbal fluidity, a line's length and form growing around his involvement with the spoken, rather than the read, poem; and an even more intense idealism. He has, also, a brilliant intensity of image, the poem shaped by his conception of material as image. His insistence on the unity of his work is an expression of the emphasis on the conception. His involvement is always as intense, always insistent on the same themes, but different in the reality that is at the base of the conception. A sunflower, a new lover, or his anger at a friend's mental breakdown will return him to his feelings of American social decay, his need for personal love, his belief in the individual necessity in opposition to the group expedient. "American Change" is just that, small coins and bills in U.S. currency, but his response to it is still another aspect of the poem that he has been so long writing.

> The first I looked on, after a long time far from home in
> mid Atlantic on a summer day
> Dolphins breaking the glassy water under the blue sky,
> a gleam of silver in my cabin, fished up out of my
> > jangling
> new pocket of coins and green dollars

Ginsberg began, as a poet, using Williams's line length and stanza form, but this looser style has some of Kerouac's sense of excitement in the immediacy of detail. The Atlantic - even on something as important as a trip back to the United States after a long absence - becomes a flash of light and glistening spray, "Dolphins breaking the glassy water under the blue sky." And with the same directness of response the poem's handful of change becomes a series of images with the same sense of excitement as his discovery of his themes within them. The nickel's the easiest, the old buffalo nickel, with its overtones of the Indian experience, the Indian loss, the failure of the American primitive to survive against the more advanced peoples who destroyed him - for Ginsberg a deepening sense of tragedy in an identification of Indian with his Jewishness. All of this in the old style nickel, and since it is only a coin held in his palm the image is not frightening. He jokes about all of it, even though there is the shared sense that none of it can really be taken as a joke.

> - held in my palm, the head of the feathered indian, old
> Buck Rogers eagle eyed jaw, a gash of hunger in the cheek
> gritted jaw of the vanished man begone like a Hebrew
> with hairlock combed down the side - O Rabbi Indian

His idealism, his response to the simplicity of other societies.

> what visionary gleam 100 years ago on Buffalo prairie
> under the molten cloud shot sky, 'the same clear light 10000
> miles in all directions'

His sense of anger at the society's sterility is touched with the dime.

> Dime next I found, Minerva, sexless cold & chill, ascend-
> ing goddess of money

In his exuberance he even finds himself questioning the goddess's sexual nature.

> executive dyke, Minerva, goddess of Madison Avenue,
> forgotten useless dime that can't buy hot dog, dead dime -

There is always the suggestibility in the poet, the responding to the object, place, moment, that turns him to some theme that is central to his attitude, but in a more subtle, complex poetic idiom this becomes less clear, the relationship less explicit. In the surrealist work of a poet like Spicer the directness of the image becomes a maze of indirection, indistinctness. The openness of Ginsberg's response to the pocketful of loose change has the simplicity of a medieval poet's symbolic imagery of flowers and plants. But in their work the language was derived second-hand, and the only freshness was in their own sudden acknowledgement of the image. In Ginsberg the language and the attitudes are entirely personal, and the excitement is direct, unabashed. And in the smallest objects he finds an image source that clarifies most of his deepest concerns. The quarter is politically sensitive, because of the Washington bust.

> Then we've George Washington, less primitive, the snub-
> nosed quarter, smug eyes and mouth, some idiot's design
> of the
> sexless Father,
> naked down to his neck, a ribbon in his wig, high fore-
> head, Roman line down the nose, fat cheeked, still showing
> his
> falsetooth ideas - O Eisenhower & Washington - O Fathers -
> No movie star dark beauty - O thou Bignoses

But it has also, for him, a personal sense of sadness. Always close to the surface in Ginsberg is the personal loss, the despair of his "Kaddish," the family tragedy of his boyhood that has never left him free as a man. Since everything is so present with him at every moment he is able to move from one emotional level to another without any shift of person or strength in the poem. It is all an expression of him, the one center in the poetry.

> nostalgia of the first touch of those coins, American
> change

and something in him that accepts the reality of the life that he had to know as a boy.

> All the struggles for those coins, the sadness of their re-
> appearance
> my reappearance on those fabled shores
> and the failure of that Dream, that Vision of Money
> reduced to this haunting recollection

> of the gas lot in Paterson where I found half a dollar
> gleaming in the grass -

The suggestibility is obvious, but it is unforced. Someone knowing Ginsberg would recognize his concerns as he fingers the handful of money, but there would still be the sense of interest in what his next response will be; since there are so many things he could respond to in any of the objects. Perhaps this is always part of the interest in a poet, like the interest in someone's opinion when they first encounter something new. The opinion is an extension of the self, and if someone is already involved with that self, as a reader of a poet has become involved in the self of the poet, then the opinion becomes important. The five dollar bill? How does it involve him? It has another President, another kind of picture and language, but instead of continuing with this imagery he shifts to something beyond the money itself. He becomes involved with the things that you can buy with a five dollar bill.

> long numbers in racetrack green, immense promise, a
> girl, a hotel, a busride to Albany, a night of brilliant drunk in
> some faraway corner of Manhattan
> a stick of several teas, or paper or cap of Heroin, or a $5
> strange present to the blind.

Then he goes back again to his handful of change, shifting the image from the things he could buy with his five dollar bill to the realization that he can just as well write poems to money itself.

> Money, money, reminder, I might as well write poems to
> you - dear American money - O Statue of Liberty I ride en-
> folded in money in my mind to you - and last

With his kind of open responding to the obvious Ginsberg has always been effective in his public poems, in the points of the poem that he reads and performs. His poem to American change ends with the details on the dollar bill, the circle,

Masonic Pyramid, serial numbers, the Eagle with "wild
wings outspread," the name of the Secretary of the Treasury,
and

> the whole surrounded by green spiderwebs designed by
> T-Men to prevent foul counterfeit
> ONE

Only someone who was sure of his attitudes toward his
society could find an imagery as coherent, as consistent, as
Ginsberg finds in his responses to something as casual as
loose money. In another poet this kind of consistency comes
from a kind of intellectual insistence, but with Ginsberg it
comes from his deep moralism. It is this, perhaps, of all the
concerns in his poetry that gives it its strongest thrust. He
insists on the moral necessity of idealism, even when he
seems to laugh at his own extravagant imagery, even when
he's writing the loose sections of the work for reading per-
formance. He has written, is writing, a long poetic expression of this morality, all of it implicit in the lines of the long
segments, "Howl" and "Kaddish," and as clearly stated, as
intensely, in the shortest poem and fragment. The poem,
from this view of it, has become Ginsberg, and he, in an
involved, complex reflection of the realities of his life, has
become his dark, tense, tangled poem.

Lawrence Ferlinghetti

"One Thousand Fearful Words For Fidel Castro"

The breath, response, the personal rhythm of Ferlinghetti's line - the immediacy, the directness of his style as he turns to tell you something. I don't think anyone else has the tone of Ferlinghetti --the flat, dry, laconic, and compelling tone - sound of his voice. If his impetus was from the French of Prevert - I think he would freely acknowledge it - his language is American, the poetry has become American.

> I am sitting in Mike's Place trying to figure out
> > what's going to happen
> > > without Fidel Castro
> Among the salami sandwiches and spittoons
> > I see no solution
> > It's going to be a tragedy
> > I see no way out

Prevert was different, even if Ferlinghetti took so much from him.

> Soyez prévenus vieillards
> soyez prévenus chefs de famille
> le temps où vous donniez vos fils à la patrie
> comme on donne du pain aux pigeons
> ce temps-là reviendra plus
> prenez-en votre parti
> c'est fini

The only acceptable translation is Ferlinghetti's.

> Be forewarned you old guys
> be forewarned you heads of families

the time when you gave your sons to the country
as one gives bread to pigeons
that time won't come again
resign yourself to it
it's over

The relationship is close - the stance has the same casual toughness - but Ferlinghetti has kept his own idiomatic style and technique. The technique of "1000 Fearful Words" is the persistent inner logic of a rhetorical device, the structure covered up with a loose, casually idiomatic poetic language. The poem - in the opening lines - implies an ignorance, an innocence, the innocence of so many other of the poets - "I'm sitting in Mike's Place trying to figure out/what's going to happen" - but the direction abruptly shifts.

I see no way out
among the admen and slumming models
and the brilliant snooping columnists
who are qualified to call Castro psychotic
because they no doubt are doctors
and have examined him personally . . .

The ignorance is only a pretense - a place to stand so he can look around him. The rhetorical technique is that of the pretended fool - his questions his own thinly veiled comment. The stance is difficult to hold long. As it moves further and further into a maze of ambiguities it becomes more and more difficult to remember every previous turning, but Ferlinghetti is too skillful to drop his pretense. The poem has an immediately effective imagery. Admen, slumming models, snooping columnists - all arouse a strong response. No one's response to them is positive, regardless of political attitudes; so he can use them in his angry defense of Fidel Castro. Castro has been called psychotic and a Communist by - columnists and admen - who are "qualified" ". . . because they no doubt are doctors." These are the people who have attacked Castro, and in his questioning attitude Ferlinghetti

78   *Some Poems/Poets*

has already made their position ridiculous, like a man who laughs at the girls in a burlesque house. Even if they ". . . know a paranoid hysterical tyrant when they see one" it is

> because they have it on first hand
> from personal observation by the CIA
> and the great disinterested news services

Their position becomes less and less tenable with every assurance of its validity. He props them up against cardboard trees that keep falling over. "First hand" - but only on the "personal observation" of the CIA, as indefensible a symbol as his slumming models. Even the little bit they know they've gotten from the "disinterested news services."

> I see no way out
> among the paisanos playing pool
> it looks like curtains for Fidel
> They're going to fix his wagon
> in the course of human events.

The incongruities of idiom, the juxtapositions of language that only someone as skilled as Ferlinghetti can pull off. After the controlled anger of the opening lines the colloquialism of "fix his wagon" and the grandiose afterthought, "in the course of human events," with its echo of the other declaration "When in the course of human events. . . ."

Someone using the figure of the fool has to position himself carefully for his questioning to be effective. He has to be sitting in the right chair at the right place at the table - or the questions will be taken too seriously. And if he's listened to that closely he has become dangerous and has to be ignored. Ferlinghetti sits in Mike's Place, with its long row of stools against a bar and some pool tables in the back of the room. Nobody will take him too seriously from his bar stool.

> In the back of Mike's the pinball machines
> shudder and leap from the floor
> when Cuban Charlie shakes them

Lawrence Ferlinghetti 79

and tries to work his will
on one named "Independence Sweepstakes"

There isn't much good contemporary political poetry. The modern idiom itself, which is personal and revelatory, with its attentions centered inward, is poorly adapted to something as public as a political poem. For the public poem you have to be able to generalize, to become almost impersonal, to find some kind of objective distance from the self. When the diction of the modern poem - the language and the syntax - is used for large generalizations it usually sounds overblown and uncomfortable. The most successful political poems using contemporary techniques seem to be personal poems, satirical or insulting, even offhand, with their point the reference to the place where the political irritation rubs against them. Often the poetry only works when there is an assumed attitude, a consciously theatrical stance, like Ferlinghetti's, with its pretense that someone else is doing all the talking. This has so sharply limited the effectiveness of political poetry that the modern poet has almost ceased to be an effective influence on anything happening in the society around him. Part of the effect of Ferlinghetti's poem is the realization that a poet has about as much social weight as his figure of the cowardly, ignorant bar fly.

They're going to fix you, Fidel
with your big Cuban cigar
which you stole from us
and your army surplus hat
which you probably also stole
and your beat beard.

Since just jeering at Castro's gotten a little tame he even shouts a little, standing up on his bar stool and looking around the room at everybody.

History may absolve you, Fidel
but we'll dissolve you first, Fidel

You'll be dissolved in history
We've got the solvent
We've got the chaser
and we'll have a little party
somewhere down your way, Fidel
It's going to be a Gas
As they say in Guatemala

Since everybody else is shouting you can say anything you
want, any reasons, justifications, just shout. A crowd in the
street that's gotten out of hand.

That's what happens, Fidel
when in the course of human events
it becomes necessary for one people to dissolve
the bonds of International Tel and Tel
and United Fruit
Fidel
Did they cut you off our frequency
We've closed down our station anyway
We've turned you off, Fidel

But it's only on the stage that the fool has to stay a fool -
and even there he can pull off his wig and wipe the lipstick
off his nose and stand revealed as someone's long-lost son or
father or uncle. He can shift his character, but at the same
moment everything he has said shifts in meaning. In the
middle of his noisy shouting Ferlinghetti suddenly steps a-
way from the attitude he assumed - throws away the costume. Behind him, as a moving force in much of his writing,
has always been an intense sympathy with the Fidel Castros
of the world, with the idealists trying to force some kind of
order on the confusion around them. He has never had any
interest in politicians, business men, police, and academi-
cians. His own idealism is an oblique expression of the same
innocence that has deeply influenced Snyder and Welch. It
is not an expression of ignorance, but a refusal to accept the
society's corruption. The questioning, noisy jeering has
taken him as far as it can in his defense of Castro - it has

Lawrence Ferlinghetti 81

questioned the validity of the criticism of him and ridiculed the war fever that wants to see Castro destroyed - ". . . we'll dissolve you first, Fidel" - but it now keeps him from making a more personal statement, from clarifying his position toward Castro and Cuba. With the sudden movement as he shifts character he alters the entire structure of the poem.

> I was sitting in Mike's Place, Fidel
> waiting for someone else to act

"was sitting" instead of the "am sitting" where the poem began. Instead of the conventional direction of the past time to present time he has gone from present to past, and with this simple reversal has pulled down the assumed attitude, the fool figure of the poem's opening. The figure he had assumed becomes an obvious pretense - if it hadn't already been clear - but, just as when the fool turns out to be somebody's cousin on the stage, everything he said has to be reconsidered. Ferlinghetti is as skilled in controlling the rhetorical movement of the poem as he is in the use of the colloquial word and phrase. Now that he has forced a complete emotional shift in the poem he is able to move, in only a few lines, to his own sense of helplessness, and the poem suddenly becomes clearly an intensely felt, an intensely personal experience.

> like a good Liberal
> I hadn't quite finished reading Camus' *Rebel*
> so I couldn't quite recognize you, Fidel
> walking up and down your island
> when they came for you, Fidel
> "My Country or Death" you told them
> Well you've got your little death, Fidel
> like an old Honest Abe

The association of Castro with Lincoln is sudden, almost forced, imposing new levels of implications, but he develops the idea into almost an elegiac mood as he uses the Lincoln figure to introduce Whitman's ode to the murdered Lincoln, with its own soft, muted overtones.

> Fidel . . . Fidel . . .
> your coffin passes by
> thru lanes and streets you never knew
> thru day and night, Fidel
> While lilacs in the dooryard bloom'd, Fidel
> your futile trip is done
> yet is not done
> and is not futile
> I give you my sprig of laurel

The fool has pulled off his wig and thrown away his striped costume and he stands crying at the edge of the stage. His sadness is even more painful, since for a moment he made us forget enough to laugh. The poem has less than its thousand words. Ferlinghetti left space for a different ending, in the chance that there could be a change in the political climate. With all its anger and its strident jeering the poem is still only another expression of the intense idealism that has shaped the poetry.

Robert Creeley

"Waiting", "The World", "Water (2)", "The Eye",
"Fragments"

I

Even when the surface of the poem is almost opaque, as
dulled in its reflections as a black marsh pool, it is difficult
not to respond to Creeley's poetry. There is always some
movement, some breaking of the surface to the emotion
below it. The surface is hard, but it isn't unyielding, and
in the poems which are less opaque his voice has a presence
and a distinctness that gives his poetry a sense of bit-
ten, hard clarity. In long reaches of his poems the hardness
gives a sense of difficulty - of difficulty with the words, the
expression, with the poem, with the emotion - and in first
encounters with Creeley's poetry there is a problem of de-
ciding if the difficulty comes from a complexity in his poetic
conception or if there is something in the poet that comes
between the poem and its language. He has said that the
poem should only be considered as the expression of its
materials - "Form is never more than an expression of con-
tent" - so it is the total intention of the poem that becomes
the point of consideration. But often the difficulty is still
there, the language with a feeling of being forced in its
struggle to become the poem. A poem that is clearly defined
in his conception of it becomes - as language - tense and
difficult. This is not only in the most guarded poem surfaces,

but in the clearer, more open poems as well. In a poem as simple as "Waiting" -

> He pushes behind the words
> which, awkward, catch
> and turn him to a disturbed
> and fumbling man

there is still a sense of strain - why the verb phrase "pushes behind"? - almost of discomfort. But instead of a confusion within the poem itself the strain seems to be a self-consciousness in Creeley's voice as he says the lines.

> What if it all stops.
> Then silence
> is as silence was
> again

Does the "it" mean his work as a poet, his consciousness of his work, the moment of the poem itself? The flatness of the statement, not even the suggestion that the "silence" could have been altered by anything he has written before. The flatness of the language - only "silence" - without an adjective - not specified, left only as "silence" with so many implications that it is left with no implication beyond its own meaning. The difficulty of the language - does Creeley intend it to be so bare? Or does the language - or the word "silence" - for him have a more implicit reference which in a personal response would give some flesh to the poem's thin bones?

> What if the last time
> he was moved to touch,
> work out in his own mind,
> such limits was the last -

The sense of the verse is interrupted momentarily with the parenthetical comment "work out in his own mind" separating "touch" and "such limits" - but still the bareness.

The implication of the opening verse is artistic inadequacy - impotence - "silence" an anguish in itself, but he doesn't allow himself pity. He doesn't even allow the poet the condescension of sympathy but forces him to confront the implications of poetic inadequacy. Not difficult within itself, not as a poetic concept, but difficult as a persistent attitude, persistent even to the blankness of a conclusion that leaves the poet with little more than the flatness of a board to sleep on and the nourishment of hard fall corn.

> God help him then
> if such things can.
> That risk
> is all there is.

II

Nothing draws him out - even a deeply felt emotion is terse and hard. Creeley is a poet who is driven to speak - but is almost unable to listen to the sound of his own voice. Not unable, since he does listen and write, but certainly guarded. And the tension of his poetic diction seems to be involved with this discomfort, not with any confusion in the poem itself. It's difficult, in many ways, to confront something as muted and withdrawn as the emotion in Creeley's poetry - it's even more difficult to realise that the poetry has in some ways become more withdrawn and more elusive as his concept of the poem has extended and deepened. Some of his writing in the 1950's had even a little of the ease and casualness of light verse.

> My wife and I lived all alone,
> Contention was our only bone.
> I fought with her, she fought with me,
> and things went on right merrily.

The later work has often an almost impenetrable emotional surface.

> As real as thinking
> wonders created
> by the possibility -

He has widened the limits of his poetry - the book *Pieces*, published in 1969, is a brilliant extended work, with a range of place and concern, of scene and accent, that gives his work an entirely new dimension - but the language is even more tightly drawn. He has thinned it down to the point where he has eliminated continuities, and the perception is left almost as word clusters - just as they must have been when they forced themselves on him. His honesty - and he is as honest as a poet as he is as a human being - can sometimes be a harrowing experience.

I don't feel at any point that Creeley is trying to make a poetic form out of emotions that are obscure or misunderstood - build a frame out of poles that are warped and splintered - or that he is trying to force poetry out of a kind of barren intellectualization that leaves the poem too heavily weighted down to have movement or direction - but that he's trying to bare himself, as a poet has to leave himself bare, as the poem at some point has to become the act of baring, and at the same time keep his bareness covered. The gestures have to be small, not move far from his body, his hands can't grasp or hold, but have to outline, suggest. The emotional power of the poems is in their half-glimpsed expression of the deeper emotion that forced him to the sudden act of baring that is the poem. The act of baring that is at the center of a poem as "The World."

> I wanted so ably
> to reassure you, I wanted
> the man you took me to be,
> to comfort you . . .

The insistent theme of his own inadequacy, from the failure as an artist that he feared in "Waiting" to a final failure as a man. The poem's opening becomes a small movement of beginning that will open out and develop. A paper tied Japanese shell that you drop in water to make blossom out into a paper flower.

> . . . to comfort you and got
> up, and went to the window,
> pushed back, as you asked me to,
> the curtain, to see
> the outline of the trees
> in the night outside

Even in this slight movement he has momentarily bared himself. In his desire to reassure he has clearly become a man who is sympathetic, as he opens the window to push back the curtains he has become a man who is involved. When the gesture is clear, direct, when the intensity of his emotions opens out with the small movements he has allowed himself the poem becomes a moving glimpse of the poet, Creeley, as he has glimpsed himself in the poem image. He has opened the window, and he stands in the darkness at the other side of the room. The poem's bareness has yielded to the stifled intensity within the concept of the poem, and its stripped thinness has become an intense emotional directness. As the poem develops its emotion takes on a more specific shape. The first lines,

> to see
> the outline of the trees
> in the night outside

have no definite implications. The movement of looking out into the night trees is in itself introspective, muted, but the introspection could be a response to so many other things. The poem's faint sound takes on a heavier resonance with its first definitions of emotional thrust, the steps across the room become a reaching out to a fuller involvement of the poet with the implications of his poem.

Robert Creeley 89

    but in the dark then
    as you slept, the grey
    figure came so close
    and leaned over
    between us, as you
    slept, reckless and

    my own face had to
    see it, and be seen by it
    the man it was, your

    grey, lost, tired, bewildered
    brother, unused, untaken
    hated by love and dead

In the darkness he has glimpsed - thought he glimpsed -
the dead brother of the woman in the room with him. The
thinness of the poem's texture had given almost a mood of
emptiness, of stillness, but it has suddenly been filled by the
grey figure Creeley senses crouching over them. In the stillness, the slackness, there is already an implication of the
loss that is death, but his immediate insistence is again of
his own inadequacy.

                for an
        instant, saw me, myself
        the intruder, as he was not

For a moment an insistence that for Creeley there is no place
that is his, no place he can stand that won't move under his
feet. Then he stops, worried, trying to explain - to give some
reason - that even if he has found himself without a place
to stand, that there is some justification for his hesitation, a
reason in the situation that is in itself a justification for his
presence.

        I tried to say, it is
        all right, she is
        happy, you are no longer

        needed . . .   .

enough of a reason to give himself time to move out of reach, only giving himself away in his anxious voice and his worried face. The effectiveness of the small movements is their interrelationship with the form of the poem. One of Creeley's greatest strengths as a poet is his nearly flawless sense of the word, its dissonances, its assonances, and its full and implied point of meaning. The strokes are short, the tonality muted, but each one is subtly placed and there is no touch that alters the tonal balance of the design. In the low murmur of the poem the stronger phrase,

> ... your
> grey, lost, tired, bewildered
> brother, unused, untaken

hangs in the air, and the sadness of "unused, untaken" has a lingering sense of melancholy. The poem has no resolution, no development of its particular moment to some larger general conception, beyond the implications of the place, the scene, itself. Within its small movements the poem could have a resolution only if Creeley were to force a shift in the context, begin talking abruptly about something else, but he doesn't move out of the shadow of the window's darkness and the still trees. The woman wakes, he tells her

> what had happened
>
> and the light then
>
> of the sun coming
> for another coming
> in the world

and the stillness sounds, in slow whispers, in the muted sadness.

III

The sense of the word - of the implications of the word. No other contemporary poet, even Williams, gives the sense of language being so honed, so pared away. The word that follows any other word in Creeley's poetry seems, in a final sense, to have been the inevitable word. Nothing else you could use would work as well. The structure of the poem, the physical form of the lines and words, has as much of this sense. He has, within his own idiom, almost perfectly achieved Emerson's discipline of form growing from argument. It is even more difficult for a poet like Creeley to have made this a workable concept; since the sparseness of his language forces the poem to turn on the implications of the verb meanings - it is what his poems do, rather than what they describe. If the verb is awkward he means to suggest awkwardness, if it is emotional he meant the emotion. "silence is as silence was. . ." "I wanted so ably to reassure you . . ." "Moved to touch . . ." The meaning is definite, even in the continued uses he makes of the simple verb "is". Many of the poems are opaque, essentially impenetrable, but only because of an unresolvable tension in the conception of the poem. The language itself has its own hard clarity. Sometimes it seems almost unnecessary to him to have anyone else read the poem. The experience is completed, and we have only a distant sight of his response to it. There are many poems like "Water (2)".

> Water drips
> a fissure of leaking
> moisture spills
> itself unnoticed

The lines themselves are no more barren than lines beginning other poems, except for the subtle suggestion of direction in the reflexive verb "spills itself" instead of the expected "spills unnoticed." But will he extend the moment of the lines, spread them out on the sidewalk like he'd unfold a piece of paper he'd found in his pocket? It has drawn a response from him, this glimpse of water dripping from a crack - but a crack in what? A wall, stone, house gutter - which? - and why has it forced itself on him?

> What
> was I looking at,
> not to see
> that wetness spread.

What he has seen was already specific in his using "spills itself", even if the poem could have gone into other directions. It is the sense of the natural experience complete within itself - almost completing itself. It is the responding to the final essence of the natural experience that gives it the distinctive mood of the Japanese haiku, but he has ended with Williams' note of laconic self-questioning. The opacity is not in the language, but in the poem itself, that he found this so intense to him that it became the hard persistence of his poem. The experience of watching water drip through a crack and spread on the ground - even if we don't know why he wanted us to have this experience the intensity of the poem has forced it on us.

IV

A poem begins,

> The eye I look out of
> or hands I use
> feet walking,
> they stay particular

The particular, in itself, can be intensely moving. In his terse, hard, difficult manner Creeley is moved by it. It is the particular moment, sight, breath that turns and returns on a kind of felt insistence that the poems must, at least, be entirely his own. In his refusal to use much of the clutter of contemporary poetic diction as a kind of impersonal concealment he has given his work its immediate identity. If he sometimes seems to limit a poem's effectiveness with the terse directness of his language the words, however muted and uneasy, are Creeley's. He goes on,

> I wanted
> one place to be
> where I was
> always.

The phrase has almost no relationship to the point where the poem began, "The eye I look out of . . . " but there is a continued wistfulness in the sense of distance he has from himself. His eyes, hands, feet, have become "they". And again the disappointment of "I wanted one place to go . . ." Each of the verses is entire within itself - stones strewn along the side of a road. Somehow he drags enough of them together to make a wall.

> I wanted you
> somehow equal
> *my* love, one says -
> I speak with that body.

"I wanted you equal." To what? To himself? It isn't clear, the small movement of the line is too abrupt, too disconnected, but the poem still moves, still has its emotional center as "my love", "that body." If his language is difficult, if he has limited the range of the poetry, he has still - with oblique strokes - sketched in a self that we can respond to - even be drawn to. In his hesitancies, in his insistence on his inadequacies, the bareness of his hopes, he has become fierce in his honesty and soft in his gentleness. And the poem does exist on this other level as an expression of the poet's self, and in our response to this self, this person, then the poem becomes an incident in the expression of this self, and we can reach through it to the poet.

> You took my heart
> which was with you,
> you took my hands
> which I used for you.

The final reality that emerges through the poetry is the person of Creeley himself, and it is this that draws us to the poems; the sympathy and sensitivity, the spare honesty and directness. And often in the poetry there can be a dual response, on one level to the person that is Creeley, and on another level to the person that is the poem. In this poem he is trying to say something about the nature of love. "You took my heart . . ." The involvement is immediate, and the poem's language, in itself, is immediate. The image is as clear in its sense of sadness as the glimpse of him in another poem opening the window to look out into the night trees. If the words insist the response is inadequate, the strength of the love is not, and the low voice, the hesitant language is only the inadequacy of speech to fill in the wiry outline of the poem's emotions.

> Oh when regrets stop
> and when silence comes
> back to be
> a place still for us,
>
> our bodies will tell
> their own story, past
> all error
> come back to us.

The poem has become Creeley's voice. Even a fragment, something like "Fragments" is important to him; since it comes out of the response and the movement of his emotions. If he seems sometimes to be unsure of his achievement - in a way that colors and shapes the form, the structure of his poetry - he is sure of his intentions. In the fragment he asks only,

> Little song, sing
> days of happiness. Make
> a pardonable wonder
> of one's blunders.

Brother Antoninus

"In The Fictive Wish"

How can a poet like Antoninus be made to fit any group of American poets or poetry? It's hard to believe that at this point there could even be an Antoninus, that somehow out of the doubt and the questioning of much American poetry of the last twenty or thirty years there could still be a poet as fervent and as stripped bare as Antoninus. He has fully invested himself in each of the dimensions of his work - from the first nature elegies that were his early response to the poetry of Robinson Jeffers to the complex, passionate poems that marked his conversion to Catholicism and his acceptance of Dominican vows. It is almost as difficult to place Jeffers' work into any kind of perspective; so it isn't surprising that the work of a disciple - as Antoninus has always described himself - has some of the same problem. The surprise is that there could *be* poetry like this being writtten.

It isn't only the insistence on the urgency of the poet's self that sets Antoninus's work apart from other poetry of the last twenty years. There have been other poets who have tried to scrape away as many layers of the skin. Antoninus, in a period when the poetic idiom has become dry and understated, has an almost seventeenth century richness of language and expression. He has a closer affinity to Vaughn, Crashaw, Alabaster - the Christopher Smart of *A Song To David* - than he does to the insistent objectivity of Robert Creeley or Denise Levertov, or to the complex allusiveness of Charles Olson or Robert Duncan. I don't think he was influenced by the metaphysical poets - he was from the beginning a Jeffers' disciple - but the feeling in the poetry is of a man, like the earlier poets, who has been driven by the torment of his life to the most intense poetry he can find language to express.

Antoninus's language is so intense, so vivid, that the poems can almost be read in clusters of words and phrases - "Far trumpets of succinctness," "a treading of feet on the stairs of redness," "I think moons of kept measure," "I felt the new wind, south/Grope her tonguing mouth on the wall," "The wind breaking its knees on this hurdle, the house," "Birds beak for her!" "In the high peal of rivering lips," "The low freighters at sea/Take in their sides the nuzzling dolphins that are their death.." He has a brilliant sense of alliteration. From *In The Fictive Wish*,

> Wader
> Watcher by water,
> Walker alone by the wave-worn shore
> In water woven.

And he doesn't hesitate to extend the flash of phrase into a poem's inner tensions. He uses a long, wavering line at points that near the stillness of a moment of contemplation. From *The Rose Of Solitude*,

> For what blooms behind your lips moves ever within my
> sight
> the kept diffusion of the smile;
> And what dawns behind your brow subsists within my
> thought
> the somnolent mystery of mind;
> And what trembles in your words lives on forever in my
> heart
> the immutable innerness of speech

But at moments of deepening intensity the line tightens to

an abrupt, insistent rhythmic unit. From earlier in *The Rose*,

> I crept
>
> I brought Him gifts
> Hushed in my heart
>
> I brought what I had
> I crept.

None of this has the flat speech rhythm that sets the dominant tone of most contemporary poetry. Duncan has his own kind of rhetorical verbosity, and Ginsberg has some of the rhythm of the synagogue chant, but the modern poet has usually been less emotional - his own responses kept at an objective distance from the poem. Antoninus has none of this restraint - the phrase, the phrase rhythm, function as a direct expression of his emotions. Part of the felt affinity with the earlier group of metaphysical poets is this emotional extravagance, this sense of poetic hyperbole. From *The Rose*,

> Heart to be hushed.
> Let it howk and then hush.
>
> Let the black wave break.
> Let the terrible tongue
> Engorge my deeps
>
> Let the loins of ferocity
> Lave my shut flesh.

From "The Song The Body Dreamed In The Spirit's Mad Behest,"

> Born and reborn we will be groped, be clenched
> On ecstasies that shudder toward crude birth,
> When His great Godhead peels its stripping strength
> In my red earth

The image and the language could almost have come from Donne's sonnet,

> Divorce mee, 'untie, or breake that knot againe,
> Take mee to you, imprison mee, for I

> Except you 'enthrall mee, never shall be free,
> Nor ever chast, except you ravish mee.

It's true that of all the contemporary poets Antoninus is the only one with some kind of persona - his identification with his holy order - that he can put between himself and his work, and it could be that this has given him the situation he needed to open his emotional stance. When he took his vows in 1951, after more than a dozen years of publication as William Everson, he had, as Brother Antoninus, a reach of expression opened to him that had been inhibited while he was still writing as William Everson. Nothing in his secular poetry has the grinding fervor of his religious writing. But is the poet William Everson? Is the poet Brother Antoninus? The two persons of Antoninus have never fully merged - even now that he has left the order and married, and the complex currents of his poetry express this continuing duality. Not confusion - I don't think there is any confusion of his separate identities in Antoninus, only a deep consciousness of their differences. But the emphasis of the poetry has moved - since 1951, when he was thirty-nine - from the preoccupations with the self to the more specific emotions of his religious self. Everson is still present in Antoninus, as the man who is Antoninus was a presence in the poems of Everson.

It is the poems from his deepest point of spiritual crisis that in some ways most intensely involve anyone reading his poetry. The poems from this point of decision, from about 1945 and 6 to 1948, have a desperate, immediate poignancy. It is possible to be unmoved by the religiosity of the later work, and to pass over the Jeffers'-like cadences of the first poems, but this period of his life was one of deep personal unhappiness, and the humanness of his loss is directly, and strongly, moving. So much seems to be slipping through his hands, and one moment of loss slides uncertain and confused into only another moment of loss. Artistically they become some of his most fully formed poems. The images of his earlier work - earth, the sea, the smells of weeds, the distances of hills and fields - have spread and extended through the lengthened lyric impulse of his dominating unhappiness. Since the poems come near his moment of crisis their resolutions are temporary - their sense of imminent despair tangled and heavy through their loping lines. *In The Fictive Wish*, from Oregon, 1946, has perhaps the most fully realized flowering of beauty, since it centers on one of his points of almost complete resolution. *The Blowing Of The Seed*, from Sebastopol, California, in 1946, is agonizing in its pained cutting of his body in its sudden despair. "There Will Be Harvest," from Berkeley the next year, in the collection *The Springing Of The Blade*, is dominated with the weight of his life's details, and its involvement with the crisis of his physical love.

In *The Fictive Wish* is a sustained lyric outburst, its syntax and form left ambiguous, but its emotional clarities brilliantly sustained. From its opening lines the difficulties of understanding are obvious, but the poem's great beauty also begins to unfold with its first hesitant breath.

> So him in dream
> Does celibate wander
> Where woman waits,
> Of whom he may come to,
> Does woman wait
> Who now is
> Of his.

Instead of "So he in dream. . ." the other pronoun form "him" for its alliteration with the final *m* of dream; the first sound of the *s* of So returning in the soft *c* of celibate, the two opening lines making a loosely conjoined phrase of four accents ending on the feminine cadence of wander. The language has an almost medieval sense of word usage in its inversions of sentence structure, "Of whom he may come to,"

"Does now the Lord retain," "Of that they then came to," and there is a suggestion of the medieval poem of physical rapture in his description of the woman's body,

> Of such body and of such croft,
> Where ache of sex could so conjoin,
> Could so sink,
> As dreams sunken;
> Of such cunted closure
> Built broad in the love grip;
> As of bed,
> Broad,
> As of width for woman;
> And of belly
> Broad for the grapple.

The language could be from Skelton, or an anonymous 15th Century carol. The poem's ending is one of his most beautifully moulded series of enfolding alliterations - the opening lines of the last section,

> Wader
> Watcher by water,
> Walker alone by the wave-worn shore,
> In water woven.

with their soft sounds of *w, wa, wo* - in the next line mingling the *w* with a beginning *m* sound

> She moves now where the wave glistens,

and in the next line it is the *m*,

> Her mouth mocking with laughter

then the *s* of glistening returns again with,

> In the slosh unheard

the sound opens to

> When the sea slurs after;
> In the sleepy suckle

and the verse ends with a long rhythmic unit developing the

l of sleepy and suckle - and leaves the sound poised for the opening line of the next verse.

> That laps at her heel where the ripple hastens,
> And the laughing look laid over her arm

The final lines are one of his most intensely moving images of loss and unhappiness.

> Lurker,
> She leaves with laughter,
> She fades where the combers falter,
> Is gone where the dream is gone
> Or the sleeper's murmur;
> Is gone as the wave withdrawing
> Sobs on the shore, and the stones are shaken
> As the ruined wave
> Sucks and sobs in the rustling stones,
> When the tide is taken.

The physical insistence of the poetry has continued since this period of his life. The pain was only briefly resolved in the certitudes of the Church. On some levels of his expression there has even been an intensification. The poetry that emerged from his years in the Dominican Order increasingly shared the violent physicality of the metaphysical poets - the acerbation of celibacy on a body that is unable to deny its desire for fulfillment. In his book *The Rose Of Solitude* the violence of desire and its turmoil becomes the central problem of the poem - and the desire expressed in the poem is open and explicit, forced in on him by the real embrace of a woman, the rose, on the floor of a San Francisco apartment,

> Now up from down under
> The long stitch of manflesh
> Goes suckering in.
>
> All that fretfulness
> Shucked now,
> Purled shuddering under.
>
> It is the make of the male.

He even questions the meanings of his continence.

> O God and Riddler,
> Why?
>
> Is this sin?
>
> I seek no sin.
> I would never offend Thee.

In an earlier verse,

> Is truly a sin
> That her name is written,
> Stroked in primal fire,
> On my stultified heart?

In "The Song The Body Dreamed In The Spirit's Mad Behest" it is a sublimated desire suffusing his response to God.

> Call Him the Lover and call me the Bride,
> Lapsing on the couch of His repose
> I heard the elemental waters rise,
> Divide and close . . .
> He is the Spirit but I am the Flesh
> Out of my body must he be reborn,
> Soul from the sundered soul, Creation's gout
> In the world's bourn . . .
> Mounted between the thermals of my thighs
> Hawklike He hovers surging at the sun,
> And feathers me a frenzy ring around
> That deep drunk tongue.

The poem has an indelible, raw energy. But in all of his mature work there has been this same sense of urgent need, and it has been as strong a force in the poems not immediately physical in their confrontations. It could be that the difference between Antoninus and most of the other poets of the last twenty years is that his blood runs closer to his skin, and that his involvement with the emotional realities of his life is more intensely felt than theirs. The guarded tone of most modern poetry does give the impression of a cautious with-drawal from a social environment so hostile that anything except a kind of guarded mistrust seems too naive as an emotional response. Whatever anyone has believed in as a kind of center for himself or the society has turned out to be mostly useless. This doesn't mean that other poets haven't been involved with the implications of sexuality, haven't brooded over the failure of what Antoninus would call Man and Woman to resolve their differences - it only means that they've decided to let less of themselves be measured against the force of this confrontation. Antoninus refuses to step out of the way, just as he has refused to deny any of the physical implications of his mature work.

At points in the poetry Antoninus seems to be over-whelmed by some of the forces he's thrust himself against. The texture of the line becomes strained, the force of the language becomes excessive. The experience of the sexual embrace is almost beyond any verbal expression, but he keeps trying to find an explicit imagery that would break through to the physical reality.

> .   .   . In my emptiness
> These arms gall for her, bride's mouth,
> Spent-breathed in laughter, or that night's
> First unblushing revealment, the flexed
> Probity of the flesh, the hymen-tilted troth,
> We closed, we clung on it, the stroked
> And clangorous rapture!

The imagery is so forced that it loses its effect of moving through to the experience itself. Sometimes his despair cries out too strongly - almost with a kind of self-indulgence.

> The face I know
> Becomes the night-black rose
>
> And I cry out of a shambling of pain,
> A clothing of anguish . . .

Brother Antoninus   105

<pre>
                    Great tongs
      Tear rents of speechlessness
      Cut from my lips . . .

      I drunkenly stagger. I flay
      Segments of numbness,
      A stuff of wretchedness
      Tatters my shanks . . .
</pre>

But the outburst is no more naked than Shelley's,

<pre>
      As thus with thee in prayer in my sore need.
      Oh, lift me as a wave, a leaf, a cloud!
      I fall upon the thorns of life! I bleed!
</pre>

Even when the imagery is most strained, the language most driven, these moments in the later work only more deeply etch the complex portrait of himself that the poetry gives us. It is poetry that meets us so strongly - even when it looms at us from directions where we hadn't expected poetry to come. And the only thing that matters now is that the poetry has come, that he has written the poems, that there is, almost unbelievably, an Antoninus.

Larry Eigner

Another Time In Fragments

I think a poet has to be useful even more than he has to be "good" - whatever good means. Useful in the sense that his poetic perception can become experience for somebody else, and I mean experience in its fullest sense of learning, feeling - using. If the poetry isn't useful to anybody it isn't kept. It isn't thrown away, since nothing that gets written and published is completely forgotten, but it's left as part of society's clutter - shoved in the back of the closet with the broken tennis rackets and the old hiking shoes. And it's more than the single poem, it's the poet's involvements - obsessions - moving into and filling out the dimensions of his experience that become the experience of the poem and the poetry. Larry Eigner's poetry - scattered through magazines and anthologies - seemed to be in pieces, the individual poems arresting in their unique style and language, but elusive and fragmentary. It was finally in the collection *Another Time In Fragments* that the poetry began to take on its larger directions, its larger implications. It was here that the poetry began to take on its sense of usefullness.

In this collection the pieces, the fragments, of Eigner's perception have become clearly the elements of an inclusive, unified world. And it is a full, complete world, even if, for most of the poems, the world extends no farther than his front porch. The front porch, the streets near the house - air, winds, trees, sounds - from the porch a world of air, birds, and the mesh of sounds around him. Living on his porch -

he is a spastic, forced to spend most of his days in a wheel chair - he has learned to see and hear with a sensitive, untiring coherence. The poems have a thinned feeling of language, a stark bare syntax, and what is left, when he has burned away the undergrowth of the poem, is the object within the poem itself, the thing that had come into his hands to be placed in the poem. As Dr. Williams had it, "No ideas, but in things." The undergrowth, in another poet's work, would be the poet's self, the identification of self, but Eigner has eliminated it for the object, which has become the poem. The spacing of his poems, as his style has matured, suggests his concentration on the things in the poem. The spaces have the feel, the shape, of the words he's cut away. Lines from almost any of the poems - #93 in *Another Time In Fragments*

        stand on one   foot
        like a tree
        the law
        is
            gulls change
            the angle

eliminate the useless words that would have involved him in the image. Anything else would have been superfluous. The poetry of China and Japan has this barrenness - and as a method of poetics has long and deep philosophic roots - but most of the younger American poets got it indirectly from the imagists, Pound, and Williams, the Williams of poems like

        Under a low sky -
        this quiet morning
        of red and
        yellow leaves -
        a bird disturbs
        no more than one twig
        of the green leaved
        peach tree

It is a poetry of the sudden glimpse, and the essence of the style is to fix the intensity of the glimpse - to find the word use, word space to give the poem the memorableness of the glimpse. If the poem is successful the two things - the poem and the moment of memory - can be almost exchanged. At least handed from one person to another, and in the exchange the poem finds its use. Eigner has found his own poetic forms to give his objects the hard lines of his awareness of them. In an earlier book, *On My Eyes*, #15, a glimpse of swimmers' heads in the glistening water beyond the beach,

> the dark swimmers
>   their heads in the sun

from *Another Time In Fragments*, #42,

> The shine was on the beach
>   and the sun is beyond in the sky

#7,

>   the
> sudden hulks of the trees
>   in a glorious summer

#81,

>   a wind
> hardly
>   to listen to

> denotes a river

Eigner's glimpses extend as he looks from one object to the next, and the relationship between the objects often becomes complex; since he doesn't explain anything. He has burned off clarification in the same move toward intensification that burned off the statement of personal involvement in the poem. The work can be difficult - without clarification - but it is compelling. The word usage that colors the object with its sudden intensity can extend to the realization of objects in relation to each other. Since he gives you only the objects you have to follow his implication of the objects to have the whole poem. It becomes like a follow-the-dots puzzle in the Sunday paper. When he gives you enough dots the image emerges with immediate clarity. An entire poem - #28 - from *Another Time*,

                 the maple
             spreads

                 perhaps
             parted by the wind
          now at an angle to
                 the wires
                     slicing

                     switchbox
                           resting there
             equal parts of
             a second or   nor'east
                                 blow

He has looked out the porch window, seen the maples that line the street spread in the wind,press back against the telephone wires running near the trees. Since it's a heavy wind he thinks of the switch box on the telephone pole and realizes that it's a gale in off the ocean. The poem has become the moment of perception itself. The image, in its placement on the page, opened out almost to give time for consideration of the poem's development, the clear glimpse that becomes the extension of experience. In poems where the involvement is less clear - where he's left out dots or left out the order they're supposed to be connected - the poem becomes more difficult. In a cluster of objects like #75 the movement from one to the others is too oblique to follow. What is the poem involved with?

```
        root
beer the good

    19 century    the American
War       crickets
  at the night the station
of the sea
```

It's hard to tell, and for its forty lines the poem holds its ground as stubbornly. At the end -

```
the outlines that yawn
      fish   live with each wave
keep your eyes when you come an
           opening ground
```

the poem has triumphed - and kept everything that might give it a meaning away from the reader. This doesn't mean that the poem isn't interesting - only that it's impossible to follow. Dr. Williams, in a letter to Robert Creeley, who had published Eigner's first book for his Divers Press, spoke of Eigner's "perfect ear," then went on, "Not that his text is not at times incomprehensible. That is a minor fault that adds piquancy to the total picture." A poem like #75 has to be useful in its glimpses, its sudden moments, since its full intention is lost. Much of Eigner's most difficult work can be opened with a reference to its positioning, to its center on his porch in Swampscott, but this is only a single aspect of the poems, and their interior reference is a complex involvement in his emotional frame at the moment of composition.

Sometimes the obscurity of a poem is a result of the directness of his creative impulse. Something has crossed his vision, or entered into range of his hearing - something read or seen - and it becomes a poem, as an almost immediate reflex of his poetic imagination. The impulse can come even from something that he's heard on the radio or seen on television. #98,

```
K    in the u s a
```

                    in black and white

                    the screen

                        what visits
                    the man pays
                        his foolish proposals
                            for the stands

If you remember Khrushchev's visit to the United States in
the 1950's the poem is immediately clear. If you don't the
peripheral notes at the final lines will be almost completely
incomprehensible.

            What we need is some more   real honest-to-gosh
                                    salesmanship

                the farmer says

                    for the cows
                        that will survive

A poem like #64, without some point of clarification, re-
mains confused and incomprehensible, despite its sugges-
tiveness.

            human
            humus

            said the arci
                        geo   anthrr

                in his large suit
                mostly it's comic
                    tomb burial
                you know, what is
                        identify

                    or else distinguished

        reference   "this gentleman

The impulse seems to be from something he's reading, but
without a reference it's difficult to get into the poem. In an-

other poem, #60, he does identify his source. The poem begins,

                that was
            the family

                        surely you believe
                    in the sky

                yes, even the palatial
                    and the rights

                "her bed and its furniture, and
            a reasonable sum but
                a gilded table
            more'n 12 ft long
                        a golden chair

It is confusing, but at the end he says, in a parenthesis, "from Eleanor of Aquitaine by Amy Kelley." With this simple movement he's made it possible to find a meaning for every element in the poem - even if to do this insists on levels of meaning more conscious than Eigner intended. In some ways - to most fully relate to the poet's own consciousness of the poem - it might be better not to know. This wouldn't keep anyone from making, and defending, elaborate systems of source identification for the poem - but it makes it more difficult for him to be sure that he's right. Eigner's poems, as a moment of his consciousness, have the intensity of that momentary experience. With each thought that becomes part of the texture of the poem there are dozens of associations and external comments. Some of them are close enough to the poem to be involved in it - in the most successful poems to deepen and amplify it - in others the relationship isn't as close. The things, words, objects, in the poem have only the involvement of being in his mind at the moment of writing. It would be misleading if someone tried to give a total coherence to all these passing inferences. Eigner is open to himself in so complete a way that anything is usable as poetic material. The best approach - with a poet who has so few exclusions - is to take the poem on this level of immediate use, and to let any of its more involved inferences develop casually from further readings.

With Eigner's work, to insist that there is a complex series of symbolic allusions through the poems is a confusion of Eigner's method of writing with the allusive poetry of an Eliot or a Hart Crane. His method - in much of the poetry - is of a series of inferences within the poem itself. The motif of the poem is developed through an involvement with the objects of the poem. As a technique it lies somewhere between Eliot's juxtaposition of ideas and Williams' "object in itself." Eigner uses the object - with the allusive inference that is specific with the object - in the kind of juxtaposition that Eliot used with ideas. A shorter poem - #34 - states the motif in its opening line,

> the knowledge of death, and now
> knowledge of the stars

The immediate sense of the second line is to involve the poem's conception of death with the more definite inference of the stars' time and space and emptiness.

> there in one end
> and the endless

> Room at the center

The definiteness of death is set against the endlessness of space, or the definite center of the space which is in itself endless. The poem has set up the drift of space and life,

> passage/in no time

The final line is only a group of objects, but he has already clarified the poem's theme of death; so each object becomes a suggestion of its own involvement with the conception of death. The objects he uses have, within this society, become a symbolic metaphor of death - could be accepted either as social allusion or as his own metaphoric language. There is probably something of the truth in both ideas.

> a rail   thickets   hills   grass

It is, beyond this kind of textual stripping, a beautiful poem, complete and intensely felt. Even within its small dimension it has almost infinite suggestion and inference. His small poems often have this sense of developing expression - developing from the concentration on the object and the multicolored spread of reference as the object moves through the intensities of his imagination.

It is the web of suggestion that spins out from Eigner's close cropping of word objects that gives the poetry its immediate use, in a sense gives it feeling of poignancy at the directness of the response to the small things like winds in off the ocean, and the large things like death in the knowledge of stars. The same structured use of object extends into most of his longer poems. Their development is only partially through the pattern of a logical thought process. #17 from *On My Eyes* is a loose sketch of a day happening around him, but its glimpsed reality is only in the sudden moments of seeing and hearing.

> IT SOUNDED
>
> and tangled dry -
>
> >   like fire
> > at the start of the day
> >   the engines
> >   control

the first suggestion is of brush fires in the neighborhood, a field burning at dawn and the fire trucks turning down his street to get to it, but it's a spring day and the sound is of wind in the dry weeds.

        but the wind in the twigs
        or thistles,   stalk

              the birds are violent
           the spring

        they function by shouting

he sees the signs of spring painting and repairing,

          the houses stand some paint in
          glass the dusty sun

          with the fresh air

          and the man who fixes the roof

          top and

the final glimpse is of boys playing on a shed, the image of
the same kind of accident - "the birds are violent" - that began the poem.

              and the boys climbing
                 the shed
              (to leap
              and break

     It is a complete day - and a specific day. It's the day he
glimpsed from the porch as the morning began with its brush
fire and ended with boys on a shed roof. The poem doesn't
have any of the common symbols of the short poem from
Another Time - it's entirely developed within his own vocabulary of object, but it has the same technical approach of
the glimpsed object used in juxtaposition with other objects,
with a cumulative effect that yields some of the emotional
experience that motivated the poem.
     Eigner's poetry is so complete, so fully realized, that I
don't think he even is concerned with the difficulty of an
American, or a vernacular discourse, in the sense that Olson
means it. The modern battle for a contemporary idiom has
been won so completely that a poet like Eigner doesn't have

to consider it. Every poem that he's published breathes in the rhythms and sounds of an American speech, and part of the sensitiveness of the poems is in their use of vernacular expression. The immediacy of an impression is most vividly communicated in an immediate poetic language, and he has always responded with the most direct speech patterns. I don't think a poet has to be "original," since a culture's responses are built into every aspect of its artistic expression, but there are poets who are so individual that their work has a strong personal identity. Eigner, I think, is one of these poets - at least he has the feeling of originality that we associate with the handful of poets whose work is extremely skilled and highly individual. No one else has so successfully combined his use of the small object within a longer, more elaborately developed poem structure. For most of the poets writing in the late 1960's the allusive detail is usually an illustration of one of the poem's concept motifs - or if it's left as itself usually the poem is short. In the intensity of his concentration Eigner is able to develop the longer poem unit, and with his sense of what Dr. Williams called his "ear" there is, at his clearest and most expressive, an underlying sense of unity, even if it's a unity made of fragments.

But Eigner's approach to the poem would be almost useless to someone else as a technique; since he writes with an emotional suddenness. The poem is conceived and written at almost the same moment. He writes many poems, and most of them have the abrupt, gesturing feel of the way they were written. The term he uses himself is "hot" - and the writing process he has described in letters is of immediate excitement in his perception.

"In ANOTHER TIME. I recall feeling successful in #14, while in #13 line 5, e.g. I just finally settled for, hopefully, the best I could manage. Sometimes such things seem pretty good after all - yeh, line 6 was, and will be, if not is, rather a strain, and seems more dubious - that's right - than line 1 of

#10. And my feeling for #12 for instance vacillates - I was happy to write it when I did."

"For a few minutes I considered putting a 1-space lacuna btwn 'ward' and 'feet' (lines 3-4) - or, that is, rather, a 1-space indent of the 4th line - but nope, the scanning association of the field of view is too fast fer that."

The objects that become his poems are already sorted in his consciousness as he writes, and the poetry is so distinct in its inclusions and its inferences that only someone who consciously imitated him could get even the same feeling of his direct, open responsiveness. A poet who is original, as Eigner is original, can't be imitated in a complete sense. An academic poet can successfully fall into the idiom and the symbolic language of another academic poet; since they have so many shared conceptions - but an Eigner's wholly individual expression is as unique as his thumbprint.

It is a ranging, full sense of the world that has to fill the poem, but Eigner's view as poet is so entire and so complete that he often seems to be unaware of the difficulty. He is involved in the moments with such intensity that he has none of the heaviness of a poet who has to think in terms of the entire range of the poetic experience. Eigner can be laconic when he is most serious, and there is an appealing freshness in his lack of pretense. The object is, after all, only itself, and if it has any other meaning it is only in the poet's conception of the object. With an object you can respond or not - and Eigner leaves you open to make the choice. At this point, when most of us distrust a heaviness, a dogmatism, of attitude or language, Eigner has an acceptable diffidence - and the opening which his poetry gives into the perception of contemporary experience has an immediate and definite use. And the sense of use, as I said at the beginning, is one of the poem's - and of poetry's - most important attributes.

Larry Eigner

Brother Antoninus

Robert Creeley

Lawrence Ferlinghetti

Allen Ginsberg

Gary Snyder

Robert Duncan

Charles Olson